LAROUSSE

POCKET GUIDE TO

KINGS & QUEENS
of Britain and Europe

D0802540

LAROUSSE

POCKET GUIDE TO
KINGS & QUEENS
of Britain and Europe

Editor
Min Lee

Assistant Editor
Mij Kelly

LAROUSSE

LAROUSSE
Larousse plc
7 Hopetoun Crescent
Edinburgh EH7 4AY

First published by Larousse plc 1995
Reprinted 1997

A CIP catalogue record for this book
is available from the British Library

ISBN 0–7523–0032–6

Typeset from author-generated disks by BPC Digital Data Ltd
Printed in England by Clays Ltd, St Ives plc

Contents

Introduction

The *Larousse Pocket Guide to Kings & Queens of Britain and Europe* sets out in the clearest possible way entries on all British kings and queens, and the most important European ones. The inclusion of European rulers helps to place the British ones firmly in their historical setting.

The alphabetical arrangement makes finding any individual very easy. For each person, the name is given in bold type, followed by birth (and death) dates. The next line states where he/she was ruler, with dates of the reign. The main entry gives an account of the main events of the reign.

For all British royal houses, and the most important European ones, family trees show the relationship of one monarch to another.

Additional information is given in the quotation boxes—either something said by the rulers, or comments about them.

Another feature of special interest is a list of people who are descendants of royal houses (and so theoretical heirs to European thrones in countries which are now republics).

The straightforward presentation makes this an ideal quick reference for anyone interested in history, at any level.

a

Adelaide (1792–1849)
Consort of William IV of Great Britain

The daughter of George, Duke of Saxe-Coburg-Meiningen. She married William, Duke of Clarence, in 1818 — 12 years before he came to the throne. Their two children died in infancy.

Adolf Frederick (1710–71)
King of Sweden (1751–71)

A descendant of King Charles XI. He was adopted as successor to King Frederick I (1743) and married Louisa Ulrika, sister of Frederick II of Prussia (1744). As king, his powers were limited by parliament during the so-called Era of Liberty. He was succeeded by his son, Gustavus III.

Agesilaus (444–360 BC)
King of Sparta (c.399–360 BC)

A brilliant soldier, he supported the Ionians against the Persian king Artaxerxes II in 397 BC and launched an ambitious campaign in Asia, but the Corinthian War recalled him to Greece, where he defeated the allied Greek forces at Coronea (394 BC).

Agis IV (3c BC)
King of Sparta (244–241 BC)

He tried to revive Sparta's military power by cancelling debts and redistributing land, but was opposed by powerful conservative interests and executed. His proposals were carried through by Cleomenes III.

Alaric I (c.370–410 AD)
King of the Visigoths (AD 395–410)

Leader of the troops who sacked Rome in AD 410 — the first time in 800 years that the city had been captured by foreigners.

Alaric II (450–507)
King of the Visigoths (485–507)

He reigned over Gaul south of the Loire, and most of Spain. In 506 he issued a code of laws known as the 'Breviary of Alaric'. He was killed at the battle of Vouillé, near Poitiers, by Clovis, King of the Franks.

Albert, Prince (1819–61)
Prince-consort of Queen Victoria of Great Britain and Ireland

The youngest son of the Duke of Saxe-Coburg-Gotha. He married his cousin Queen Victoria in 1840, and became her chief advisor, first as Consort (1842), then as Prince Consort (1857). He encouraged the arts and social and industrial reforms, and it was largely on his initiative that the Great Exhibition of 1851 took place.

Albert I (1875–1934)
King of the Belgians (1909–34)

The nephew of Leopold II, whom he succeeded. He gained respect for his resistance to the German occupation of 1914–18 and for his conduct during the subsequent restoration. He died while rock climbing and was succeeded by his son, Leopold III.

Albert I (c.1255–1308)
King of Germany (1298–1308)

The son of Rudolf I of Habsburg. Following his election as king, he defeated and killed the deposed king, Adolf of Nassau, in battle at Göllheim and set about restoring the power of the monarchy. He was murdered while crossing the River Reuss by his nephew John.

Alboin (d.574)
King of the Lombards (561–74)

He fought against the Ostrogoths and in 568 invaded Italy, establishing Pavia as the Lombard capital. He was generally considered to be a just ruler, but at a feast in Verona he made his queen drink from her father's skull, and she persuaded her lover to murder him.

Alexander I (c.1077–1124)
King of Scots (1107–24)

The son of Malcolm Canmore and Queen (later St) Margaret. He succeeded his brother Edgar and ruled north of the Forth–Clyde line, while his younger brother David (later David I) controlled S Scotland in his name. He maintained friendly relations with England by marrying Sybilla, an illegitimate daughter of Henry I, and also fought alongside Henry in Wales (1114).

Alexander II (1198–1249)
King of Scots (1214–49)

He succeeded his father, William the Lion, supported the English barons against John, and later made a peace treaty with Henry III (1217). He gave up his claims to Northumberland, Cumberland, and Westmorland by the Treaty of York (1237), and asserted royal authority in the north and west of Scotland. His reign was a landmark in the establishment of the kingdom of Scotland.

Alexander III (1241–86)
King of Scotland (1249–86)

The son of Alexander II, whom he succeeded. He married Margaret, daughter of Henry III of England (1251), defeated King Haakon IV of Norway at Largs (1263) and strengthened his hold on the west of Scotland. His reign has been seen as a golden age for Scotland, during which the king's authority was unquestioned and trade flourished. He died in a cliff-fall, riding at night between Burntisland and Kinghorn, leaving only his infant grand-daughter, Margaret of Norway, to succeed him.

Alexander I (1777–1825)
Tsar of Russia (1801–25)

The son of Paul I, whom he succeeded. He immediately initiated a wide range of reforms and in 1805 Russia joined the coalition against Napoleon, but following a series of military defeats was forced to agree the Treaty of Tilsit (1807) with France. When Napoleon broke the treaty by invading Russia in 1812, Alexander pursued the French

back to Paris. He claimed and received Poland at the Congress of
Vienna (1815).

> Napoleon thinks that I am a fool, but he who laughs last laughs
> longest.
>
> *1808 Letter to his sister, 8 Oct*

Alexander II, the Liberator (1818–81)
Tsar of Russia (1855–81)

The son of Nicholas I, whom he succeeded. His achievements included
the emancipation of the serfs (1861), local government, legal and
military reforms, the extension of the Russian Empire into central
Asia and the Far East, and the defeat of Turkey in the war of
1877–8. He was assassinated in St Petersburg and was succeeded by
his son, Alexander III.

> It is better to abolish serfdom from above than to wait for it to
> abolish itself from below.
>
> *1856 Speech, 30 Mar*

Alexander III (1845–94)
Tsar of Russia (1881–94)

The younger son and successor of Alexander II. Openly critical of his
father's reforming policies before he came to the throne, Alexander
followed a repressive policy in home affairs, especially in the
persecution of Jews, and promoted Russian language and traditions
and the Orthodox Church. Abroad, he strengthened Russia's hold on
central Asia. He was succeeded by his son Nicholas II.

Alexander I (1888–1934)
King of the Serbs, Croats and Slovenes (1921–9), and of
Yugoslavia (1929–34)

The second son of Peter I. He was commander-in-chief of the Serbian
army in World War I and regent for his father (1914–21). He tried
to build a strong and unified Yugoslavia, imposing a royal dictatorship
in 1929. He was assassinated in Marseilles by a terrorist in the pay of
Croatian nationalists.

Alexander, the Great or Alexander III (356–323 BC)
King of Macedonia (336–323 BC)

The son of Philip II and a pupil of Aristotle. He crushed all opposition at home, then conquered Persia in a series of battles: Granius (334 BC), Issus (333 BC), and Gaugamela (331 BC). He conquered Egypt and founded the city of Alexandria, consulting the oracle of Ammon at Siwah Oasis (which apparently encouraged his belief in his divine descent). By 330 BC, Darius III of Persia had fled, and the capitals of Babylon, Susa, Persepolis, and Ecbatana had been taken. In the next three years, he conquered the eastern half of the Persian empire then set out to invade India (327 BC). He conquered the Punjab, but was forced to return when his troops mutinied. He died shortly after in Babylon.

Alexandra of Denmark (1844–1925)
Queen-consort of Edward VII of Great Britain

The eldest daughter of Christian IX of Denmark. She married Edward in 1863, when he was Prince of Wales. She did much charity work, and was particularly involved in the support of nursing and hospitals.

Alexey I (1629–76)
Tsar of Russia (1645–76)

The son and successor of Michael Romanov. His court was notorious for its splendour and excess. Abroad, he waged war against Poland (1654–67), regaining Smolensk and Kiev, while at home his attempts to reduce the power of the Orthodox church brought him into conflict with the Patriarch, Nikon. In 1649 he legitimized peasant serfdom, and in 1670–1 suppressed a great peasant revolt. He was the father of Peter I, the Great.

Alfonso I, the Battler (1073–1134)
King of Leon and Castile (1104–34)

The King of Leon through his marriage with its queen, Urraca, he freed Saragossa from Moorish rule in 1118.

Alfonso III, the Great (d.910)
King of Leon, Asturias, and Galicia (866–910)

He fought over 30 campaigns and gained numerous victories over the
Moors, occupied Coimbra, and extended his territory as far as
Portugal and Old Castile. He was dethroned by his three sons.

Alfonso V, the Magnanimous (1396–1458)
King of Leon, Castile and Sicily (1416–58)

The son of Ferdinand I, whom he succeeded. In 1442, after a long
contest, he made himself king also of Naples.

Alfonso VIII (1155–1214)
King of Castile (1158–1214)

His long struggle against the Muslim dynasty of the Almohads was
hindered by quarrels with Alfonso IX of Leon. However, in alliance
with Aragon and Navarre, and with papal support, he won the victory
of Las Navas de Tolosa (1214), which severely weakened Muslim
power and paved the way for the eventual reconquest of southern
Spain.

Alfonso X, the Astronomer or the Wise (1221–84)
King of Leon and Castile (1252–82)

The son of Ferdinand III, whom he succeeded. He captured Cadiz
and Algarve from the Moors, and thus united Murcia with Castile. A
poet and philosopher, his great code of laws and his planetary table
are famous. A rising led by his son Sancho robbed him of his throne.

> Had I been present at the Creation, I would have given some useful
> hints for the better ordering of the universe.
>
> *Attrib, on studying the Ptolemaic system*

Alfonso I or Affonso Henriques (c.1110–85)
King of Portugal (1139–85)

Only two years old at the death of his father, Henry of Burgundy, he
later seized power from his mother (1128), defeated the Moors at
Ourique (1139), and proclaimed himself the first King of Portugal.
He took Lisbon (1147), and later all Galicia, Estremadura, and Elvas.

Alfonso V or Affonso el Africano (1432–81)
King of Portugal (1438–81)

The son of Duarte, whom he succeeded. He received his surname in
honour of his conquests in North Africa. He tried without success to
unite Castile with Portugal, but gave up his claim in the Treaty of
Alcaçovas, after which Portugal's interests were directed towards
expansion in Africa.

Alfonso XII (1857–85)
King of Spain (1874–85)

The son of Isabella II. He was proclaimed king following the
overthrow of his mother by the army in 1868, and a period of
republican rule. With the final overthrow of the Carlists (supporters
of the Spanish pretender Don Carlos de Bourbon) and constitutional
reform, his reign was a time of peace and relative prosperity.

Alfonso XIII (1886–1941)
King of Spain (1886–1931)

The son of Alfonso XII and Maria Christina of Austria. His reign was
increasingly authoritarian and unpopular. After neutrality during
World War I, the Spanish were defeated by the Moors in Morocco
in 1921. From 1923 he associated himself with the military
dictatorship of Primo de Rivera (1923–30). When, in 1931, his
people voted overwhelmingly for a republic, he refused to abdicate,
but left Spain, and died in exile.

Alfred, the Great (849–99)
King of Wessex (871–99)

The fifth son of King Ethelwulf. When he came to the throne the
Danes had already conquered Northumbria, East Mercia and East
Anglia, and were threatening Wessex itself. He defeated them at the
battle of Edington, in Wiltshire (878), and began to win back Danish-
occupied territory by taking London (886) and by organizing his
forces into a standing army, building a navy and setting up a network
of burgs (fortified centres). He made links with other English peoples
not under Danish rule and paved the way for his successors to
reconquer the Danelaw. The story of his being scolded by a peasant
woman for letting her cakes burn was first recorded in the 11c.

Ancus Marcius (640–616 BC)
Traditionally the fourth King of Rome

He is said to have conquered the neighbouring Latin tribes, and settled them on the Aventine.

Anna Ivanovna (1693–1740)
Empress of Russia (1730–40)

The daughter of Ivan V and niece of Peter the Great. After the early death of Peter II she was elected to the throne by the Supreme Council under conditions that severely limited her power. She responded by abolishing the council, and with her German favourite, Ernst Johann Biron, established a reign of terror in which 20,000 people are said to have been banished to Siberia.

Anne (1665–1714)
Queen of Great Britain and Ireland (1702–14)

The daughter of James II, and sister of Mary II. In 1683 she married Prince George of Denmark (1653–1708). Only one of their 17 children, William, Duke of Gloucester (1689–1700), survived infancy. The influence of Lord Churchill (later Duke of Marlborough) and his wife Sarah Jennings was powerfully felt in all public affairs during the greater part of Anne's reign, which was marked by the union of England and Scotland (1707), and the long struggle against Louis XIV of France known as the War of the Spanish Succession. The Marlboroughs (with Godolphin) headed the Whig Party, but Anne quarrelled with them and then found a new favourite in Abigail Masham, under whose influence she appointed a Tory government (1710). She was the last Stuart monarch; on her death the throne passed to George I of Hanover.

Anne of Austria (1601–66)
Wife of Louis XIII of France

The eldest daughter of Philip III of Spain. Her marriage to Louis XIII (1615) was unhappy, the royal couple living for the first 22 years in a state of virtual separation (due chiefly to the influence of Cardinal Richelieu). Anne was regent (1643–51) for her son Louis XIV.

Anne of Bohemia (1366–94)
Queen-consort of Richard II of England.

The daughter of Emperor Charles IV, and first wife of Richard II, whom she married in 1382. She died of the plague.

Anne of Cleves (1515–57)
English queen, the fourth wife of Henry VIII

A Lutheran princess, her marriage to Henry (Jan 1540) was part of an English strategy to develop an alliance with German Protestant rulers. The marriage was declared null and void six months afterwards. Anne agreed to the divorce, accepting a large income.

> I see nothing in this woman as men report of her.
>
> *Henry VIII*

Anne of Denmark (1574–1619)
Wife of James VI of Scotland, later James I of England

The daughter of Frederick II of Denmark, she married James in 1589. She was a lavish patron of the arts.

Antigonus Gonatas (c.320–239 BC)
King of Macedonia (276–239 BC)

The son of Demetrius Poliorcetes. It took him seven years to regain the throne of his father in 276 BC. He defeated an invasion of Gauls in the winter of 279–278 BC and defended his kingdom against several rivals, including Pyrrhus of Epirus. The dynasty he founded lasted until the Roman conquest in 167 BC.

Archelaus
King of Macedonia (413–399 BC)

A great patron of the arts.

Arsinoe II (316–271 BC)
Macedonian princess

The daughter of Ptolemy I. She married first the aged Lysimachus, King of Thrace (c.300 BC), and finally her own brother, Ptolemy II Philadelphus (c.276 BC). Several cities were named after her.

Arthur (6c)
Semi-legendary King of the Britons

A champion of Christianity, he is described as having united the British tribes against pagan invaders. His story is told in many medieval romances, and various legends became interwoven with it, including those of the Round Table and the Holy Grail. His origins are variously claimed to have been in Brittany, Cornwall, and Wales, but it is possible that the historical Arthur was a Romanized Britain who led a force against Saxon invaders.

Athelstan or Aethelstan (c.895–939)
King of England (927–39)

The first King of all England, son of Edward the Elder, and grandson of Alfred, the Great. Acknowledged as King of Wessex and Mercia (924), he built upon his predecessors' achievements by invading Northumbria and bringing all of England under his rule.

Attila (c.406–53 AD)
King of the Huns (AD 434–53)

Known as the 'Scourge of God', Attila extended his empire from the Rhine to the frontiers of China. He invaded Gaul in AD 451, and though defeated there he invaded Italy in AD 452, where Rome itself was saved only by the intervention of Pope Leo I, who bribed Attila with large sums of money.

Augustus II, the Strong (1670–1733)
King of Poland (1697–1704, 1709–33)

He succeeded his brother, John George IV, as elector of Saxony in 1694. With Peter I (the Great) of Russia and Frederick IV of Denmark, he planned the partition of Sweden, but was defeated by Charles XII of Sweden. He was deposed in 1704 and replaced by Stanisław Leszczyński, but recovered the Polish throne in 1709. He was succeeded, both as elector and king, by his son, Frederick Augustus.

b

Balliol, Edward (c.1283–1364)
'King' of Scotland (1332–56)

The elder son of John Balliol, and rival claimant to the throne of David II. In 1332 he landed with 3,400 followers at Kinghorn in Fife. On 12 August, he surprised and routed the Scottish army under the new regent, the Earl of Mar, at Dupplin Moor in Perthshire. On 24 September he was crowned king of Scotland at Scone. Less than three months later, he was himself surprised at Annan and fled across the Border on an unsaddled horse. His claim to the throne of Scotland was supported by Edward III of England, who restored his title to him in 1333 after victory in the Battle of Halidon Hill. Balliol kept his title despite the return to Scotland in 1341 of David II, but he remained under the power of Edward III, to whom he finally resigned his claim in 1356.

Balliol, John (c.1250–1315)
King of Scotland (1292–6)

Nicknamed 'Toom Tabard' or 'Empty Jacket' by the Scots. On the death of Margaret, the 'Maid of Norway' in 1290, he claimed the crown of Scotland, and his claim was supported by Edward I of England over that of Robert Bruce. Balliol was crowned at Scone (1292) and swore loyalty to Edward, renouncing the guarantees of Scottish liberties of the Treaty of Bingham (1290). By 1295 a council of 12 Scottish magnates had taken control of government out of his hands and made an alliance with France, then at war with England. Edward invaded Scotland, took Balliol prisoner, and forced him to surrender his crown on 10 July 1296.

Battenberg, Prince Alexander of (1820–93)
First prince of Bulgaria (1879–86)

The son of Prince Alexander of Hesse, and the nephew of Alexander II of Russia. He was elected prince of the new principality of Bulgaria in 1879. In 1885 he took control of eastern Romania, triggering a war with Serbia, whose army he swiftly defeated. He was forced to abdicate by pro-Russian army conspirators.

Baudouin I (1930–93)
King of the Belgians (1951–93)

The elder son of Leopold III and his first wife, Queen Astrid. He came to the throne on the abdication of his father, and in 1960 married the Spanish Dona Fabiola de Mora y Aragon. He was succeeded by his brother, Albert II.

Beatrix (Wilhelmina Armgard) (1938–)
Queen of the Netherlands (1980–)

The eldest daughter of Juliana and Prince Bernhard zur Lippe-Biesterfeld. In 1966 she married the German diplomat Claus-Georg Wilhelm Otto Friedrich Gerd von Amsberg (1926–) and in 1980 came to the throne on the abdication of her mother. Their son, Prince Willem-Alexander Claus George Ferdinand (1967–) is the first male heir to the Dutch throne in over a century. There are two other sons: Johan Friso Bernhard Christiaan David (1968–) and Constantijn Christof Frederik Aschwin (1969–).

Berengar I (d.924)
King of Italy (from 888) and Holy Roman Emperor (from 915)

He succeeded his father Eberhard, a count of Frankish origin, as margrave of Friuli. He died at the hands of his own men.

Berengar II (c.900–66)
King of Italy (950–61)

The grandson of the King of Halzand, Berengar I. He succeeded his father as margrave of Ivrea (928) and was crowned king in 950. In 961 he was dethroned by the emperor Otto I and after three years' refuge in a mountain fortress was sent as a prisoner to Bavaria where he died.

Bethlen Gabor (Gabriel Bethlen) (1580–1629)
King of Hungary (1620–1)

Born into a Hungarian Protestant family, he was elected prince of

Transylvania in 1613. In 1619 he invaded Hungary and had himself elected king in 1620.

Boabdil or Abu-Abdallah Muhammad (d.c.1493)
King of Granada (1482–92)

He dethroned his father, Abu-al-Hasan, in 1482. While he continued to struggle for power against his father and uncle, the Christians gradually conquered the kingdom. Malaga fell in 1487, and in 1492 Ferdinand and Isabella of Aragon and Castile took Granada. He was granted a lordship in the Alpujarras, but in 1493 sold his rights to the Spanish crown.

Boadicea see Boudicca.

Boleyn, Anne (c.1504–36)
English queen, the second wife of Henry VIII

Secretly married to Henry (Jan 1533), she was soon declared his legal wife (May). His quickly cooling passion for her was not revived by the birth (Sep 1533) of a princess (later Elizabeth I), still less by that of a stillborn son (Jan 1536). She was charged with treason and beheaded (19 May), and Henry married Jane Seymour 11 days later.

> I now think the King so much in love that only God can get him out of this mess.
>
> *1528 Letter from Jean du Bellay to Francis I*

Bonaparte, Jérôme (1784–1860)
King of Westphalia (1807–13)

The son of Charles and Marie Bonaparte, and brother of Napoleon. He was sovereign of Westphalia from July 1807 to October 1813, marrying Princess Catherine of Württemberg in August 1807. After exile, he returned to Paris in 1847. His nephew Napoleon III created him a Marshal of France, and consulted him over the strategy of the Crimean War. Jérôme's great-grandson Louis, Prince Napoleon, born in 1914, became head of the House of Bonaparte in 1926.

Bonaparte, Joseph (1768–1844)
King of Naples and Sicily (1806–8) and Spain (1808–13)

The eldest surviving son of Charles and Marie Bonaparte, and brother of Napoleon. He served Napoleon on diplomatic missions and was a

humane sovereign in southern Italy, but faced continuous rebellion
as a nominated ruler in Spain where his army was decisively defeated
by Wellington at Vitoria (June 1813).

Bonaparte, Louis (1778–1846)
King of Holland (1806–10)

The son of Charles and Marie Bonaparte, and brother of Napoleon.
He married Napoleon's step-daughter, Hortense Beauharnais, in
1802. He ruled Holland as King Lodewijk I, abdicating in 1810 after
Napoleon complained that he was too concerned about the interests
of his Dutch subjects. He was the father of Napoleon III.

Boris Godunov (1552–1605)
Tsar of Russia (1598–1605)

An intimate friend of Ivan the Terrible, who entrusted to him the
care of his feeble son, Theodore. During the reign of Tsar Theodore
(1584–98), Godunov was virtual ruler of the country, becoming tsar
himself on Theodore's death. He continued the expansionist policies
of Ivan, going to war against both Poland and Sweden. During the
last years of his reign he was involved in a civil war against a pretender,
who claimed to be Dmitri, the younger son of Ivan the Terrible.

Boudicca or Boadicea (1c AD)
Queen of the Iceni

A British warrior-queen, wife of Prasutagus, King of the Iceni, a tribe
who inhabited what is now Norfolk and Suffolk. On her husband's
death (AD 60), the Romans seized her territory, and treated the
inhabitants brutally. She gathered a large army, destroyed the Roman
colony of Camulodunum (modern Colchester), took Londinium
(London) and Verulamium (St Albans), and put to death as many as
70,000 Romans. Defeated in battle by Suetonius Paulinus, she
committed suicide.

Brian (c.926–1014)
King of Ireland (1002–14)

Known in the annals as 'Brian Boroimhe' or 'Boru' (Brian of the
tribute). In 976 he became chief of Dál Cais, and after much fighting
he made himself king of Leinster (984). Further campaigns led to his

rule being acknowledged over all Ireland. He was killed after defeating the Vikings at Clontarf.

Bruce, Robert, or Robert I (1274–1329)
King of Scotland (1306–29)

Hero of the Scottish War of Independence. Shortly after renewing an oath of loyalty to Edward I in 1297, he joined the Scottish revolt under William Wallace. He killed John Comyn, the nephew of Balliol and a rival with a better claim to the throne, and two months later he was crowned king at Scone. He was forced to flee Scotland after two military defeats in 1306, but returned to defeat an English force at Loudoun in May 1307. Edward I was succeeded the following July by his weaker son, Edward II, and by 1309 Robert was able to hold his first parliament. He enjoyed spectacular military success between 1310 and 1314, and although the victory at Bannockburn, near Stirling, over a larger English army of nearly 20,000 men on 24 June 1314 did not end the Anglo-Scottish war, it did virtually settle the Scottish civil war, leaving Robert I unchallenged. The Declaration of Arbroath, written in 1320 by his chancellor, Bernard de Linton, and a mission to Avignon, finally persuaded Pope John XXII to recognize Robert as king in 1323. A truce with England brought hostilities to an end in 1323, but Robert took advantage of the accession of the young Edward III in 1327 to force the Treaty of Northampton (1328), which secured English acknowledgement of Scottish independence and his own right to the throne. According to legend, when outlawed by the English, Robert restored his hope and patience by watching a spider weave its web.

Brunhilde (567–613)
Frankish queen

The daughter of the Visigothic king Athanagild and wife of King Sigbert of Austrasia. She ruled as regent for her two grandsons, Theodebert II, King of Austrasia, and Theodoric II, King of Burgundy, over the whole Frankish world along with her rival Fredegond, who governed Neustria for the young Clotaire II. On Fredegond's death in 598 she seized Neustria, and for a time ruled over the whole Merovingian dominions, but she was overthrown by the Austrasian nobles under Clotaire II, and put to death by being dragged behind a wild horse.

C

Cadwallon (d.634)
King of Gwynedd (c.625–34)

A pagan Welsh king, in 633 he invaded the Christian kingdom of Northumbria with Penda, King of Mercia, and killed King Edwin at the battle of Heathfield (Hatfield Chase) near Doncaster. He ravaged the kingdom but was himself defeated and killed by King Oswald (St Oswald) of Bernicia at the battle of Heavenfield near Hexham.

Canute or Cnut (c.995–1035)
King of England (from 1016), Denmark (from 1019), and Norway (from 1028)

The younger son of Sweyn Forkbeard, after whose death (1014) he challenged Ethelred the Unready and Edmund Ironside for the English throne. He defeated Edmund in 1016 at the battle of Assandun, secured Mercia and Northumbria, and became king of all England after Edmund's death. The story of his failure to stop the tide coming in was invented by the 12c historian Henry of Huntingdon.

Capet, Hugo or Hugh (c.938–96)
King of France (987–96)

Founder of the third Frankish royal dynasty (the Capetians), which ruled France until 1328. The son of Hugh the Great, whom he succeeded as Duke of the Franks in 956, he was elected king and crowned at Noyon (987). His 40 years in power were marked by constant political intrigue and struggle.

Carl XVI, Gustaf (1946–   )
King of Sweden (1973–   )

The grandson of King Gustavus VI. Since his father had died in an air accident (1947), he became Crown Prince when his grandfather came to the throne (1950). A new constitution limiting monarchical powers was approved by the Swedish parliament just before his accession (1973). In 1976 he married Silvia Sommerlath (1943–　). They have three children: Victoria (1977–　), who is heir to the Swedish throne, Carl Philip (1979–　), and Madeleine (1982–　).

Carol I (1839–1914)
King of Romania (1881–1914)

He was made Prince of Romania in 1866 and when his country received independence from the Ottoman Empire he became its first king. He carried out many reforms, but was unable to prevent the peasant revolt of 1907, when many thousands were killed.

Carol II (1893–1953)
King of Romania (1930–40)

The eldest son of King Ferdinand I and great-nephew of Carol I. His flamboyant private life created constant problems. In 1917 he married a commoner, Zizi Lambrino, whom he divorced to marry Princess Helen of Greece in 1921 and by whom he had a son, King Michael. In 1925 he renounced his right of succession to the throne, deserted his wife, and went into exile with his mistress, Magda Lupescu. In 1930 he returned to Romania and became king, overthrowing his son. His reign was made chaotic by pressures from both Russia and Germany, and in 1940 he was deposed through German influence in favour of his son, and fled into exile in Spain.

Caroline of Ansbach (1683–1737)
Queen-consort of George II of Great Britain

The daughter of a German prince. She exercised a strong influence over her husband, and was a leading supporter of his chief minister, Robert Walpole.

Caroline of Brunswick, Amelia Elizabeth (1768–1821)
Wife of George IV of Great Britain

The daughter of George III's sister, Augusta. She married George, Prince of Wales, in 1795 and bore him a daughter (Princess Charlotte). However, at his request they lived apart. When George became king (1820), she refused the offer of an annuity to renounce the title of queen, but although his divorce bill failed, she was not allowed into Westminster Abbey at the coronation (Jul 1821).

> Most Gracious Queen, we thee implore
> To go away and sin no more,
> But if that effort be too great,
> To go away at any rate.
>
> *1820 Epigram quoted in a letter from Francis Burton to
> Lord Colchester, 15 Nov*

Cassander (c.354–c.297 BC)
King of Macedonia (305–c.297 BC)

The son of Antipater. He put to death Olympias, the mother of Alexander the Great; also Roxana (Alexander's wife) and her children; and married Thessalonica (Alexander's half-sister), for whom he built and named a city in Macedonia.

Catherine I (1684–1727)
Empress of Russia (1725–7)

A Roman Catholic of lowly birth, she converted to Orthodoxy in 1708 and Tsar Peter I married her in 1712, following her distinguished conduct while on campaign with him. He named her as his successor, and when she came to the throne on his death in 1725, she continued her husband's reforms. She was succeeded by Peter's grandson, Peter II.

Catherine II, the Great (1729–96)
Empress of Russia (1762–96)

In 1745 she began an unhappy marriage to the heir to the Russian throne (later Peter III). She spent much of her time in political intriguing and extra-marital affairs, until a palace coup overthrew her husband and she was proclaimed empress. Her energetic foreign policy included the extension of the Russian Empire south to the Black Sea as a result of the Russo-Turkish Wars (1774, 1792), and in the west she brought about the three partitions of Poland. In 1774 she suppressed the popular rebellion led by Pugachev, and later actively persecuted members of the progressive-minded nobility.

> I shall be an autocrat: that's my trade. And the good Lord will
> forgive me: that's his.
>
> *Attrib*

Catherine de' Medici (1519–89)
Queen of France, wife of Henry II

The daughter of Lorenzo de' Medici, Duke of Urbino. She was married at 14 and, on the death of her husband, acted as queen regent (1559–63) during the minority of her sons Francis II and Charles IX. As queen mother she continued to influence Charles. With the state torn by religious wars, she was drawn into political intrigues, and advised the slaughter of Parisian Huguenots in the infamous St Bartholomew's Day Massacre (1572).

Catherine of Aragon (1485–1536)
English queen, the first wife of Henry VIII

The fourth daughter of Ferdinand and Isabella of Spain. She was first married in 1501 to Arthur (1486–1502), the eldest son of Henry VII, and after his early death married his young brother Henry (1509). Of their five children, only the Princess Mary (later Mary I) survived. In 1527 Henry began a procedure for divorce and in 1533 he married Anne Boleyn, thereby breaking with the pope and triggering the English Reformation. Catherine retired to lead a religious life.

Catherine of Braganza (1638–1705)
Queen-consort of Charles II of England

The daughter of John IV of Portugal. She was married to Charles in 1662 as part of an alliance between England and Portugal, but she was unable to produce an heir. She helped to convert Charles to Catholicism just before his death, after which she returned to Portugal (1692).

Catherine of Valois (1401–37)
Queen of England, wife of Henry V

The daughter of King Charles VI of France. She married Henry V after a stormy courtship, when England and France went to war over Henry's dowry demands. In 1421 she gave birth to the future Henry VI. After her husband's death in 1422, she secretly married Owen Tudor, a Welsh squire — their eldest son, Edmund, Earl of Richmond, was the father of Henry VII, the first of the Tudor kings of England.

Charlemagne or Charles the Great (742–814)
King of the Franks (from 771) and Emperor of the West (from 800)

The eldest son of Pepin the Short. He defeated the Saxons (772–804), the Lombards (773–4), fought the Arabs in Spain, and took control of most of Christian W Europe. In 800 he was crowned emperor by Pope Leo III. In his later years, a period that has become known as the 'Carolingian Renaissance', he strengthened his vast empire, promoting Christianity, education, agriculture, the arts, manufacture, and commerce.

> Charlemagne was by far the most able and noble-spirited of all those who ruled over the nations in his time.
>
> *Einhard*, Vita Caroli, *written between 829 and 836*

Charles I (1600–49)
King of Scotland and England (1625–49)

The second son of James VI and I and Anne of Denmark. His marriage to the French princess Henrietta Maria (1625) caused religious unease, as the marriage Articles allowed her to follow her Catholic religion. Three parliaments were summoned and dissolved in the first four years of his reign, then for 11 years Charles ruled without one. He warred with France (1627–9), and in 1630 made peace with Spain, but his continuing need for money led to unpopular economic policies. His unpopularity increased when he attempted to anglicize the Scottish Church (1639). In 1642 Charles entered into the Civil War, but he suffered a severe defeat at Naseby (14 Jun 1645), and surrendered to the Scots at Newark (1646). After many negotiations, and a second Civil War (1646–8), he came to trial at Westminster, where his refusal to plead was seen as a confession of guilt. He was beheaded (30 Jan 1649).

Charles II (1630–85)
King of Scotland and England (1660–85)

The son of Charles I. He was forced into exile during the Civil War. On his father's execution (1649), he was crowned king at Scone (1651) and marched on England, but his forces met defeat at Worcester (1651). He remained in exile until summoned back as king (1660). In 1662 he married the Portuguese princess Catherine of Braganza, who bore him no heir, though Charles was the father of many illegitimate children. His war with Holland (1665–7) was unpopular, and led to the dismissal of his adviser, Lord Clarendon. However, he negotiated skilfully between conflicting political and religious pressures, including the trumped-up 'Popish Plot'. He was succeeded by his brother James.

> Here lies a great and mighty king
> Whose promise none relies on:
> He never said a foolish thing,
> Nor ever did a wise one.
>
> *Lord Rochester's epitaph*

Charles I (1887–1922)
Emperor of Austria and King of Hungary, as Charles IV (1916–18)

He became heir presumptive to both thrones on the assassination (1914) of his uncle, Archduke Francis Ferdinand, and then succeeded his great-uncle, Francis Joseph (1916), but was compelled to abdicate in 1918. Two attempts at restoration in Hungary (1921) failed, and he died in exile in Madeira.

Charles I, the Bald (823–77)
King of France (from 843) and Emperor of the West (as Charles II, from 875)

The son of Louis the Pious and grandson of Charlemagne.

Charles II, the Fat (839–88)
King of France (884–8), King of Germany (882–7) and Emperor of the West (as Charles III, 881–7)

The son of Louis the German, and grandson of Louis the Pious. He was deposed as Holy Roman Emperor after making a humiliating treaty with the Vikings in Paris in 887.

Charles III, the Simple (879–929)
King of France (893–922)

He was deposed after surrendering Normandy to the Vikings under Rollo.

Charles IV, the Fair (1294–1328)
King of France (1322–8)

He was the last of the Capetian dynasty.

Charles V, the Wise (1337–80)
King of France (1364–80)

He acted as regent during the captivity of his father, John II, after the battle of Poitiers (1356). During his reign, he regained most of the territories lost to the English.

Charles VI, the Foolish (1368–1422)
King of France (1380–1422)

The son of Charles V, whom he succeeded. From 1392 he suffered from fits of madness. He was defeated by Henry V of England at the battle of Agincourt (1415).

Charles VII, the Victorious (1403–61)
King of France (1422–61)

The son and successor of Charles VI. When he came to the throne, the north of the country was in English hands, with Henry VI proclaimed king of France. Joan of Arc inspired the French to end the English siege of Orléans (1429) and though she was later captured and executed, the French continued victorious, regaining nearly all the land lost to the English under Charles VI.

Charles VIII, the Affable (1470–98)
King of France (1483–98)

The son of Louis XI, whom he succeeded. In 1495–6 he failed in an attempt to secure the kingdom of Naples.

Charles IX (1550–74)
King of France (1560–74)

The second son of Henry II and Catherine de' Medici, he succeeded his brother, Francis II. His reign coincided with the Wars of Religion, and he was largely controlled by his mother. Her influence led him to authorize the slaughter of the Parisian Huguenots in the St Bartholomew's Day Massacre (1572).

Charles X (1757–1836)
King of France (1824–30)

The grandson of Louis XV and the last Bourbon king of France. He married Maria Theresa of Savoy in 1773 and lived in England during the French Revolution. He returned to France as Lt-General (1814) and succeeded his brother Louis XVIII (1824), but his repressive rule led to revolution, and his eventual abdication and exile.

Charles IV (1316–78)
King of Germany (from 1347) and Holy Roman Emperor (from 1355)

The son of King John of Bohemia. Unlike his predecessors, as Holy Roman Emperor he tried to avoid being drawn into Italian conflicts. Instead, through shrewd diplomacy, he built up a dynastic empire based round his hereditary lands of Bohemia and Moravia. His *Golden Bull* of 1356 became the new constitutional framework for the empire. He was succeeded by his son, Wenceslas IV.

Charles V (1500–58)
Holy Roman Emperor (1519–56) and King of Spain (as Charles I, 1517–56)

The son of Philip of Burgundy and Joanna of Spain. His defeat of Francis I of France in 1525 led to the formation of an alliance against him by Pope Clement VII, Henry VII, Francis and the Venetians. In 1527 Rome was sacked and the pope imprisoned, and although Charles disclaimed any part of it, the Peace of Cambrai (1529) left him master of Italy. At the Diet of Augsburg (1530) he confirmed the 1521 Edict of Worms, which had outlawed Martin Luther, and when, in 1538, he agreed a 10-year truce with Francis and the pope, the Protestants rebelled. They were crushed at Mühlberg (1547), but in 1552 Charles was defeated by Maurice of Saxony, and Protestantism received legal recognition. In 1555 he divided the Empire between his son (Philip II of Spain) and his brother (Emperor Ferdinand I).

> To God I speak Spanish, to women Italian, to men French, and to my horse — German.
>
> *Attrib*

Charles II (1661–1700)
King of Spain (1665–1700)

The son of Philip IV. Although he joined the Grand Alliance against Louis XIV of France, he nevertheless named Louis's grandson, Philip of Anjou, as his successor in his will, thereby causing the War of the Spanish Succession. His reign marked the end of Spanish power in Europe.

Charles III (1716–88)
King of Spain (1759–88)

The younger son of Philip V, and half-brother of Ferdinand VI, whom he succeeded. During the Seven Years War (1756–63) he sided with France against Britain and lost Florida, but regained it in 1783 by siding with the Americans during the War of Independence (1775–83). At home he reformed the nation's economy, strengthened the crown's authority over the church, and expelled the Jesuits. He was succeeded by his son, Charles IV.

> Everything for the people, nothing by the people.
>
> *His maxim*

Charles IV (1784–1819)
King of Spain (1788–1808)

The son of Charles III. His government was largely controlled by his wife Maria Louisa and her favourite, Manuel de Godoy. Nelson destroyed his fleet at Trafalgar, and in 1808 he abdicated under pressure from Napoleon, in favour of Napoleon's brother Joseph.

Charles VIII (1408–70)
King of Sweden (1448–57, 1464–5, 1467–70) and of Norway (1449–50)

A powerful Swedish magnate, he was elected king of Sweden on the death of Christopher of Bavaria. A year later he was elected king of Norway. He lost the Norwegian throne immediately to Christian I of Denmark, and in 1457 was driven from Sweden by an uprising in favour of Christian. He was twice recalled to the throne before his death in 1470.

Charles IX (1550–1611)
King of Sweden (1604–11)

The youngest son of Gustavus I, half-brother of Erik XIV, and uncle
of Sigismund III Vasa of Poland and Sweden. In 1568 he helped to
depose Erik XIV and place their brother Johan III on the throne. A
champion of Lutheranism, he resisted the Counter-Reformation
promoted by Johan III and his son and successor Sigismund III, and
deposed Sigismund in 1598. He was involved in wars with Poland
(1600–10) and Denmark (1611–13). He was succeeded by his son,
Gustavus II.

Charles X (1622–60)
King of Sweden (1654–60)

An outstanding soldier, he succeeded to the throne on the abdication
of his cousin, Queen Kristina. He forced the elector of Brandenburg
to acknowledge his overlordship of Prussia, and crushed the Polish
forces in a terrible three-day battle at Warsaw (1656). During his
war with the Danes (1657–8), he crossed the Little and Great Belt
on the ice in one of the most daring exploits in military history and
seized Zealand. He was succeeded by his son, Charles XI.

Charles XI (1655–97)
King of Sweden (1660–97)

The son of Charles X, whom he succeeded. In 1675 he helped to halt
a Danish invasion and in the aftermath of the war he trimmed the
power of the nobility and reorganized the armed forces. In 1693 he
was granted almost absolute monarchical power, with which he
carried out far-reaching reforms in the administration of the country.
He was succeeded by his son, Charles XII.

Charles XII (1682–1718)
King of Sweden (1697–1718)

The son and successor of Charles XI. When Denmark, Poland and
Russia formed an alliance against him, he attacked Denmark (1699),
compelling the Danes to ask for peace, then defeated the Russians at
Narva (1700), and dethroned Augustus II of Poland (1704). He
invaded Russia again in 1707, and was eventually defeated at Poltava
(1709). He escaped to Turkey but in 1714 returned to launch an

attack on Norway. He was killed at the siege of Halden, leaving his
country exhausted by war.

> I have resolved never to begin an unjust war, but also never to end
> a just war without overcoming my enemy.
>
> *1700 To his council*

Charles XIII (1748–1818)
King of Sweden (from 1809) and of Norway (from 1814)

The younger brother of Gustavus III. When his nephew Gustavus IV
Adolf was deposed in 1809 he was elected king, agreeing a new
constitution limiting the powers of the monarchy. In the following
year he adopted the French marshal Bernadotte (later Charles XIV)
as his successor.

Charles XIV (1763–1844)
King of Sweden and Norway (1818–44)

Born Jean Baptiste Jules Bernadotte. He joined the French army as a
common soldier in 1780 and by 1799 was Minister of War. After
fighting in several Napoleonic campaigns (1805–9), in 1810 he was
elected heir to the throne of Sweden, when he changed his name to
Charles John. He helped to defeat Napoleon at Leipzig (1813), and
in 1814 secured a union between Norway and Sweden that lasted
until 1905.

Charles XV (1826–72)
King of Sweden and Norway (1859–72)

The son and successor of Oskar I. He promised to support Denmark
in her border disputes with Germany, but when Denmark declared
war on Germany in 1864 the Swedish government refused to honour
the king's pledge. During his reign the old Riksdag of the four Estates
was replaced in 1865–6 by a Riksdag of two chambers with equal
rights. He was succeeded by his younger brother, Oskar II.

Charles Albert (1798–1849)
King of Sardinia-Piedmont (1831–49)

The son of Prince Charles Emmanuel of Savoy-Carignan. Briefly
appointed regent in 1821, he was soon arrested and exiled by the
new king, Charles Felix, whom he later succeeded. He introduced

many liberal reforms, but in 1848 declared war on Austria, and was soundly defeated at the battle of Novara (1849) and soon after abdicated in favour of his son Victor Emmanuel II.

Charles of Anjou (1227–85)
Angevin King of Naples and Sicily (1265–85)

The son of Louis VIII of France. After defeating rival claimants, Manfred, King of Sicily (1266), and Conradin of Swabia (1268), he established control of the kingdom. He conquered Corfu and much of mainland Greece, and planned to capture Constantinople, but his plans were wrecked by a revolt which began in Sicily in 1282 (the Sicilian Vespers). This enabled Manfred's son-in-law, Peter III of Aragon, to seize Sicily.

Charles Robert (1288–1342)
King of Hungary (1310–42)

On the death of Andrew III (1301) he claimed the throne (through his mother) and, following a struggle with rival claimants, was crowned. He restored royal authority by creating a new and loyal aristocracy, and reorganized the army. He married Elizabeth, daughter of Casimir III of Poland, and in 1337 obtained recognition of his son, the future Louis the Great, as heir also to the Polish throne.

Charlotte Sophia (1744–1818)
Queen-consort of George III of Great Britain and Ireland

She married George III in 1761, shortly after he came to the throne, and bore him 15 children. Their eldest son was the future George IV.

Christian I (1426–81)
King of Denmark (1448–81), Norway (1450–81), and Sweden (1457–1464)

The son of Dietrich, Count of Oldenburg. He succeeded Christopher III as king of Denmark. In 1450 he evicted Charles VIII of Sweden from the throne of Norway, and from 1457 to 1464 he evicted Charles from the Swedish throne as well. He was succeeded by his son, John I.

Christian II (1481–1559)
King of Denmark, Norway (1513–23) and Sweden (1520–3)

The son of John I. His treacherous massacre of the Swedish nobles (8–10 Nov 1520) caused such outrage that he was driven out by Gustavus I Vasa in 1523, marking the end of the Kalmar Union between the three kingdoms. In Denmark a popular revolt placed his uncle, Frederick I, on the throne. Totally defeated at Akershus in 1532, he spent his remaining years a prisoner.

Christian III (1503–59)
King of Denmark and Norway (1534–59)

The elder son and successor of Frederick I. He came to the throne in the midst of a civil war (1533–6) between his Protestant supporters and the Catholic supporters of the ex-king Christian II. He established the Lutheran state church and hugely strengthened the monarchy. His son, Frederick II, succeeded him.

Christian IV (1577–1648)
King of Denmark and Norway (1588–1648)

The son of Frederick II, whom he succeeded. He engaged in two wars against Sweden (1611–13, 1643–5) and took part in the Thirty Years War, joining the Protestant Union in 1625 to help his niece, Elizabeth of Bohemia. However, he withdrew from the conflict after a catastrophic defeat in 1626 shattered Denmark's power and prestige.

Christian VII (1749–1808)
King of Denmark and Norway (1766–1808)

The son and successor of Frederick V. In 1766 he married Caroline Matilda, sister of King George III of Britain, and in 1784 was declared insane. His son, Crown Prince Frederick, became regent and eventually succeeded him as Frederick VI.

Christian VIII (1786–1848)
King of Denmark (1839–48)

The son and successor of Frederick VI. He was elected king of Norway in 1814, but was promptly deposed when Norway was taken by Charles XIV of Sweden. As king of Denmark he granted Iceland a consultative assembly and freedom of trade. Early in 1848 he signed an order abolishing the absolute powers of the monarchy, which was implemented by his son and successor, Frederick VII.

Christian IX (1818–1906)
King of Denmark (1863–1906)

He succeeded the childless Frederick VII. The November Constitution of 1863, which incorporated Schleswig into the Danish kingdom, led to war with Prussia and Austria and the loss of both Schleswig and Holstein. In 1874, he granted Iceland's first constitution, of limited autonomy under a governor. He was succeeded in 1906 by his elder son, Frederick VIII.

Christian X (1870–1947)
King of Denmark (1912–47)

During the German occupation (1940–5), he remained in Denmark and worked to save his country from the harshest effects of occupation. He was succeeded by his son Frederick IX.

Christina see Kristina.

Cleomenes I (d.490 BC)
King of Sparta (c.520–490 BC)

He drove the Pisistratid dynasty from Athens in 510 BC and tried repeatedly, and unsuccessfully, to bring Athens under Spartan influence. He arranged the overthrow of his fellow king Demaratus in 491 BC by bribing the Delphic oracle, but his deceit was discovered and he fled from Sparta.

Cleomenes III (c.260–219 BC)
King of Sparta (235–222 BC)

Inspired by the example of Agis IV, he carried out (in 227 BC) a programme of reforms to increase the number of citizens and make Sparta once again leader of the Peloponnese. His success alarmed the Achaean League, who routed his army at Sellasia in 222 BC.

Clotaire I or Chlotar (6c)
King of the Franks

The son of the Frankish king Clovis, he inherited the kingdom jointly with his three brothers in 511, but gradually added to his lands until, with the death of his brother Childebert I in 558, he became ruler of all the Franks.

Clotaire II (d.628)
King of the Franks (613–28)

The grandson of Clotaire I. He came to power in 613 after a period of regency, recovered lost territories and extended his rule over all the Franks.

Clovis I (c.465–511)
King of the Franks (481–511)

The son of Childeric, whom he succeeded. He overthrew the Gallo-Romans, and by AD 496 had taken possession of the whole country between the Somme and the Loire. In AD 493 he married (St) Clotilda, and after routing the Alemanni was converted to Christianity along with several thousand warriors. In 507, he defeated the Visigoth Alaric II, captured Bordeaux and Toulouse, but was checked at Arles by the Ostrogoth, Theodoric.

Conrad I (d.918)
King of Germany (911–18)

The son of the Count of Franconia, and nephew of the Emperor Arnulf. He re-established imperial authority over most of the German princes, conducted an unsuccessful war with France, and died at Quedlinburg in a battle with the Hungarians.

Conrad II (c.990–1039)
King of Germany (from 1024) and Holy Roman Emperor (from 1027)

The son of the Duke of Franconia. He crushed a rebellion in Italy, but was soon recalled to Germany to put down four revolts. In 1033 he was crowned king of Burgandy. A second rebellion recalled him to Italy (1036), where he was forced to grant his Italian subjects various privileges. He was succeeded by his son Henry III.

Conrad III (1093–1152)
King of Germany (1138–52)

The son of Frederick of Swabia. In 1125 he unsuccessfully contested the crown of Italy with the emperor Lothar III, after whose death the

princes of Germany offered Conrad the throne. He was immediately
involved in a quarrel with Henry the Proud, Duke of Bavaria and
Saxony, the struggle being continued under Henry's son, Henry the
Lion. He was succeeded by his nephew, Frederick I Barbarossa.

Constantine I (1841–1929)
King of Greece (1913–17, 1920–2)

After playing a leading part in the Balkan Wars (1912–13), he
succeeded his father George I as king. During World War I, his policy
of neutrality led to conflict with forces led by liberal politician
Venizelos, resulting in virtual civil war (1916–17), Anglo-French
intervention, and his abdication. Restored after the war, he abdicated
once again (1922), following Greece's defeat by Turkey and an
internal military revolt.

Constantine II (1940–)
King of Greece (1964–73)

The son of Paul I, whom he succeeded. In 1964 he married Princess
Anne-Marie of Denmark (1946–). He fled to Rome (Dec 1967),
following a military coup, and was officially deposed in 1973. The
monarchy was abolished by a national referendum in 1974.

Cymbeline or Cunobelinus (d.c.43 AD)
King of the Catuvellauni tribe (c.10–c.43 AD)

A pro-Roman king, he ruled most of SE Britain from his capital at
Camulodunum (Colchester). Shakespeare's Cymbeline was loosely
based on Holinshed's half-historical Cunobelinus.

ᚥ

David I (c.1080–1153)
King of Scots (1124–53)

The youngest son of Malcolm Canmore and Queen (later St) Margaret. During his reign he laid the foundations of the medieval kingdom of Scotland. In 1136 he supported the claims of his niece, Empress Matilda, to the English Crown, and went to war against Stephen. He was defeated in 1138 at the battle of the Standard, near Northallerton, but from 1141 occupied the whole of N England to the rivers Ribble and Tees.

David II (1324–71)
King of Scots (1329–71)

The only surviving son of Robert Bruce. He became king at the age of five, and was crowned at Scone in 1331. After Edward III of England defeated David's guardian at Halidon Hill (1333), Edward Balliol of Scotland became de facto king under the influence of Edward III. David fled to France until 1341. He later invaded England, but was captured at Neville's Cross (1346) and imprisoned for 11 years. He was succeeded by his sister's son, Robert II.

Dagobert I (605–39)
King of Austrasia (from 623)

The son of Clotaire II. From 629 he ruled over a combined Frankish kingdom and subsequently set his sons over Neustria and Austrasia. He was the last Merovingian king to hold significant power.

Dagobert II (d.679)
King of Austrasia, (676–9)

The son of Sigibert III, after whose death in 656 he was banished to an Irish monastery. He was recalled and made king in 676, but was assassinated after a short reign.

Demetrius Poliorcetes, the Besieger (d.283 BC)
King of Macedonia (294–288 BC)

The son of Antigonus Monophthalmos. He was expelled (288 BC) and died the prisoner of Seleucus I.

Diniz, Denis (1261–1325)
King of Portugal (1279–1325)

He founded the University of Lisbon (1290); made the first commercial treaty with England (1294); formed the Portuguese navy (1317); introduced improved methods of agriculture; and was both a patron of literature and music and a prolific poet.

e

Edgar (943–75)
King of Mercia and Northumbria (from 957) and of all England (from 959)

The younger son of Edmund I. To increase his prestige and power, he encouraged the reform of the English Church, but his lavish support for the monasteries caused bitterness among the nobility. In c.973 he introduced a uniform currency based on silver pennies.

Edmund I (921–46)
King of the English (939–46)

The half-brother of Athelstan, whom he succeeded. When he came to the throne, Scandinavian forces from Northumbria, reinforced by levies from Ireland, quickly overran the E Midlands. He re-established control over the S Danelaw (942) and Northumbria (944), and then ruled a reunited England.

Edmund II, Ironside (c.980–1016)
King of the English (1016)

The son of Ethelred the Unready. He was chosen king by the Londoners on his father's death (Apr 1016), while Canute was elected at Southampton by the Witan (Council). Edmund hastily raised an army, defeated Canute, but was routed at Ashingdon (or possibly Ashdon), Essex (Oct 1016). He agreed to a partition of the country, but died a few weeks later, leaving Canute as sole ruler.

Edmund, St (c.841–70)
King of East Anglia (855–70)

According to tradition, the son of a Frankish king. When the Danes invaded East Anglia in 870, Edmund met them at Hoxne, in Suffolk, and was defeated and taken captive. It is said that when he refused to renounce his Christian faith, he was tied to a tree and shot to death with arrows by the pagan Danes.

Edward I (1239–1307)
King of England (1272–1307)

The elder son of Henry III and Eleanor of Provence. He married Eleanor of Castile (1254) and later Margaret of France, the sister of Philip IV (1299). In the Barons' War (1264–7), he at first supported Simon de Montfort, but rejoined his father, and defeated de Montfort at Evesham (1265). He then won renown as a crusader to the Holy Land, and after his return (1274) took N and W Wales, where he built several castles to mark his conquests. On the death of Margaret, the 'Maid of Norway', he chose John Balliol to occupy the vacant Scottish throne (1292). Although Balliol swore loyalty to Edward the Scottish magnates forced him into an alliance with France (1295), then at war with England. Thus began the Scottish Wars of Independence, and despite prolonged campaigning and victories such as Falkirk (1298), Edward could not subdue Scotland as he had done Wales.

> Edward I was a brave, wise and resourceful ruler, enterprising and very successful in war.
>
> *Froissart*, Chronicles, *written between 1369 and 1373*

Edward II (1284–1327)
King of England (1307–27)

The fourth son of Edward I and Eleanor of Castile. In 1301 he was created Prince of Wales, the first English heir apparent to bear the title, and in 1308 married Isabella of France, the daughter of Philip IV. Throughout his reign, Edward mismanaged the barons, who wanted to rid the country of royal favourites and regain their place in government. He invaded Scotland in 1314 but was defeated by Robert Bruce at the battle of Bannockburn (1314). Risings followed in Wales and Ireland. Taken captive (1326) by his wife, Queen Isabella, and her lover, Roger Mortimer, Edward was forced to abdicate in favour of his eldest son, and afterwards was murdered in Berkeley Castle.

Edward III (1312–77)
King of England (1327–77)

The elder son of Edward II and Isabella of France. He married Philippa of Hainault in 1328, and their eldest child Edward, later called the Black Prince, was born in 1330. By banishing his mother from court and executing her lover, Roger Mortimer, he took control of the government (1330) and began to restore the monarchy's authority and prestige. He supported Edward Balliol's claim to the throne of Scotland, defeating the supporters of David II at Halidon Hill (1333). In 1337, he laid claim to the French Crown through his mother Isabella (the daughter of Philip IV), thus beginning the Hundred Years War. He destroyed the French navy at the battle of Sluys (1340), and won another major victory at Crécy (1346). He was succeeded by his grandson, Richard II.

Edward IV (1442–83)
King of England (1461–70, 1471–83)

The eldest son of Richard, Duke of York. His father claimed the throne as the descendant of Edward III's third and fifth sons (Lionel, Duke of Clarence, and Edmund, Duke of York), against the Lancastrian King Henry VI (the descendant of Edward III's fourth son, John of Gaunt). Richard was killed at the battle of Wakefield (1460), but Edward entered London in 1461, was recognized as king when Henry VI was deposed, and with the support of his cousin Richard Neville, Earl of Warwick, defeated the Lancastrians at Towton. In 1470 Warwick turned against him, forcing him into exile in Holland, and restoring Henry VI to the throne. Edward returned to England (Mar 1471), regained kingship (11 Apr), defeated and killed Warwick at the battle of Barnet (14 Apr), and destroyed the remaining Lancastrian forces at Tewkesbury (4 May). Henry VI was murdered in the Tower soon afterwards, and Edward remained secure for the rest of his reign.

Edward V (1470–83)
King of England (Apr–Jun 1483)

The son of Edward IV and Elizabeth Woodville. Shortly after his father's death, he and his younger brother Richard, Duke of York, were imprisoned in the Tower by their uncle Richard, Duke of Gloucester, who seized the throne as Richard III. The two princes were presumably murdered (Aug 1483) on their uncle's orders.

Edward VI (1537–53)
King of England (1547–53)

The son of Henry VIII and Jane Seymour. During his reign, power was first in the hands of his uncle the Duke of Somerset, and then of John Dudley, Duke of Northumberland. Edward became a devout Protestant, and under the Protectors the English Reformation flourished. He died of tuberculosis, having named Lady Jane Grey as his successor.

Edward VII (1841–1910)
King of the United Kingdom (1901–10)

The eldest son of Queen Victoria. In 1863 he married Alexandra (1844–1925), the eldest daughter of Christian IX of Denmark. They had six children: Albert Victor (1864–92), Duke of Clarence; George (1865–1936), later George V; Louise (1867–1931), Princess Royal; Victoria (1868–1935); Maud (1869–1938), who married Haakon VII of Norway; and Alexander (born and died 1871). While he was Prince of Wales, his behaviour caused considerable scandal, and the Queen excluded him from affairs of state. As king, he carried out several visits to European capitals to improve international relations.

> Because a man has a black face and a different religion from ours, there is no reason why he should be treated as a brute.
>
> *1875 Letter from India to Lord Granville, 30 Nov*

Edward VIII (1894–1972)
King of the United Kingdom (Jan–Dec 1936)

The eldest son of George V. He succeeded his father in 1936, but abdicated because of his proposed marriage to Wallis Simpson, an American who had been twice divorced. He was then given the title of Duke of Windsor, and the marriage took place in France in 1937. They lived in Paris, apart from a period in the Bahamas (1940–5), where Edward was Governor.

> I have found it impossible to carry the heavy burden of responsibility and to discharge my duties as King as I would wish to do without the help and support of the woman I love.
>
> *1936 Radio broadcast to the nation following his abdication to marry Wallis Simpson, 11 Dec*

Edward the Confessor (c.1003–66)
King of England (1042–66)

The elder son of Ethelred the Unready and Emma of Normandy, and the last king of the Old English royal line. He succeeded his half-brother Hardicanute to the throne, and until 1052 held his position against the ambitious Godwin family by building up Norman favourites. Though in 1051 the childless Edward probably recognized Duke William of Normandy (later William I) as his heir, the Godwins regained their influence and on Edward's death he was succeeded by Harold Godwin (Harold II) — the Norman Conquest followed soon after. Edward was canonized in 1161.

Edward the Elder (c.870–924)
King of Wessex (899–924)

The elder son of Alfred the Great. He became the strongest ruler in Britain, for in a great military campaign he conquered the S Danelaw (910–18), and assumed control of Mercia (918). In 920, his overlordship was recognized by all the chief rulers beyond the Humber, including the King of Scots.

Edward the Martyr (c.962–78)
King of England (975–8)

The elder son of Edgar, whom he succeeded. Rival claims on behalf of his younger half-brother Ethelred the Unready led to his murder at Corfe, Dorset, by supporters of his stepmother, Elfrida. He was canonized in 1001.

Edwin (584–633)
King of Northumbria (616–33)

He united Northumbria, pushed his power west as far as the islands of Anglesey and Man, obtained the overlordship of East Anglia, and (by a victory over the West Saxons) of all England, apart from Kent. He was converted to Christianity, and baptized with his nobles in 627. He fell in battle against Mercians and Welsh at Hatfield Chase, and was afterwards canonized.

Egbert (d.839)
King of Wessex (802–39)

Following his victory in 825 over the Mercians at Ellendun (now
Wroughton) in Wiltshire, he gained control of Essex, Kent, Surrey
and Sussex. His conquest of Mercia itself (829) was short-lived, but
he extended his control over Cornwall and defeated the allied Vikings
and Britons at Hingston Down (838). These successes made him
master of S England from Kent to Land's End, and established Wessex
as the strongest Anglo-Saxon kingdom.

Eleanor of Aquitaine (c.1122–1204)
Queen-consort first of Louis VII of France and then of Henry II of England

Following the annulment of her marriage to Louis VII (1152), she
married Henry Plantaganet, who in 1154 became Henry II of England.
She was imprisoned (1174–89) for supporting the rebellion of her
sons, two of whom became kings as Richard I (in 1189) and John (in
1199).

Eleanor of Castile (c.1245–1290)
Queen-consort of Edward I of England

The daughter of Ferdinand III, she married the future Edward I in
1254. She accompanied Edward to the Crusades, and is said to have
saved his life by sucking the poison from a wound. She died at Harby,
Nottinghamshire, and the 'Eleanor Crosses' at Northampton,
Geddington, and Waltham Cross are survivors of the 12 erected by
Edward at the halting places of her cortège. The last stopping place
was Charing Cross, where a replica now stands.

Elizabeth I (1533–1603)
Queen of England (1558–1603)

The daughter of Henry VIII and Anne Boleyn. On the death of Edward
VI (1553) she sided with her half-sister Mary (later Mary I) against
Lady Jane Grey and the Duke of Northumberland, but her
Protestantism made Mary suspicious, and she was imprisoned for her
supposed part in the rebellion of Wyatt (1554). She came to the

throne on Mary's death and, guided in her government by William Cecil as Secretary of State, established herself as a strong but tolerant Protestant monarch, making peace with France and Scotland. Later the formal establishment of the Anglican Church and the imprisonment of Mary, Queen of Scots (1568) caused endless plots among English Catholics. Elizabeth eventually had Mary executed (1587), and she persecuted the Catholics and supported the Dutch rebellion against Philip of Spain — leading him to attack England, unsuccessfully, with his Armada (1588). Considered a strong, cruel, and capricious woman, the 'Virgin Queen' was nevertheless popular with her subjects. Her reign is seen as the period when England became a world power.

> I know I have the body of a weak and feeble woman, but I have the heart and stomach of a king — and a king of England too.
>
> *1588 Address at Tilbury on the approach of the Spanish Armada*

Elizabeth II (1926–)
Queen of Great Britain and Northern Ireland and Head of the Commonwealth (1952–   )

The elder daughter of George VI. Married in 1947, her husband is Prince Philip, Duke of Edinburgh. They have three sons, Charles Philip Arthur George (1948–), Andrew Albert Christian Edward (1960–), and Edward Anthony Richard Louis (1964–), and a daughter, Anne Elizabeth Alice Louise (1950–). When she was a child, there seemed little prospect of her acceding to the throne until her uncle, Edward VIII, abdicated in favour of her father. When in 1951 the health of King George VI deteriorated, Princess Elizabeth Alexandra Mary represented her father at various state occasions, including the Trooping of the Colour. She was proclaimed Queen on 6 Feb 1952 and after the three months full mourning for her father, she undertook the routine duties of the sovereign. She was crowned on 2 Jun 1953. She has been the first reigning British monarch to visit Australia and New Zealand (1953), South America (1968) and the Persian Gulf countries (1979), as well as undertaking the first royal British tour of the Indian subcontinent for 50 years (1961). She is a keen horsewoman, and by virtue of her financial and property holdings, one of the richest women in the world.

Elizabeth Petrovna (1709–62)
Empress of Russia (1741–62)

The daughter of Peter the Great and Catherine I. She came to the throne on the deposition of Ivan VI. During her reign she made peace with Sweden and, fuelled by her rivalry with Frederick the Great, became involved in the War of the Austrian Succession and in the Seven Years War.

Elizabeth, the Winter Queen (1596–1662)
Queen of Bohemia

The eldest daughter of James VI and I of Scotland and England and Anne of Denmark. She married (1613) Frederick V, elector palatine, a champion of the Protestant cause. As a result of his brief, unhappy winter as king of Bohemia, Elizabeth became known variously as 'the Winter Queen' or 'the Queen of Hearts' and became a symbol of the Protestant cause in Europe. Her son, Charles Louis, was restored to the palatinate in 1648.

Erik Blood-axe (d.954)
King of Norway (942–7) and of the Viking kingdom of York (948–54).

The eldest son of Harold I Fine-hair, whom he succeeded. His violent reign in Norway ended when he was deposed by his youngest brother, Haakon I. He fled to England, where he became king in York of the Norse realm in Northumbria, but was eventually expelled in 954 and killed in battle at Stainmore in Yorkshire.

Erik, the Saint (12c)
King of Sweden (c.1155–95)

The patron saint of Sweden. He is said to have led a Christian crusade for the conversion of Finland; also to have been murdered at mass in Uppsala by a Danish pretender to his throne.

Erik VII (Erik of Pomerania) (1382–1459)
King of Denmark, Sweden (1397–1438) and Norway (1397–1442)

The son of Duke Wratislaw VII of Pomerania and Maria, niece of Queen Margaret, he was adopted as heir to the triple monarchy by his great-aunt, in 1389. His aggressive commercial and military policies against the Hanseatic League led to economic disasters and eventual rebellion, and he was deposed in all three countries one by one. He was succeeded by his nephew, Christopher of Bavaria.

Erik XIV (1533–77)
King of Sweden (1560–9)

The eldest son of Gustavus I, whom he succeeded. In 1563 he imprisoned his half-brother Johan for treason and launched a seven-year war against Denmark for control of the Baltic ports, which ended inconclusively with the Peace of Stettin (1570). Increasingly mentally unstable, he married a soldier's daughter, Karin Månsdotter, whose coronation as queen in 1568 provided an excuse for rebellion. Erik was dethroned in favour of his brother, Johan III, and died in captivity, probably of arsenic poisoning.

Ermanaric or Jörmunrekkr (4c)
King of the Ostrogoths

He built up a huge empire centred on the Dnieper, but was overthrown by the Huns, and may have committed suicide when wounded. In Germanic legend he is described as a cruel tyrant who had his wife trampled to death by wild horses, and was mortally wounded by her brothers in a suicidal revenge attack.

Ernest Augustus (1771–1851)
King of Hanover (1837–51)

The fifth son of George III. He entered the Hanoverian army (1790); lost his left eye at Tournay (1794); was created Duke of Cumberland (1799); and in the House of Lords showed himself a strong Tory and staunch Protestant. In 1837 under the Salic law he succeeded William IV as King Ernest I of Hanover, while Victoria (the only child of Ernest's brother Edward) succeeded to the throne of Great Britain.

Ethelbert (c.552–616)
King of Kent (560–616)

During his reign Kent gained (c.590) control over England south of the Humber, Christianity was introduced by St Augustine (597), and English laws were written down for the first time.

Ethelred or Aethelred I (c.830–71)
King of Wessex (865–71)

The elder brother of Alfred the Great. During his reign the Danes
launched their main invasion of England, and he died soon after his
victory over them at Ashdown, Berkshire.

Ethelred or Aethelred II, the Unready (c.968–1016)
King of England (978–1016)

The son of Edgar. He ascended the throne as a boy, after the murder
of his half-brother, Edward the Martyr. An alliance with Normandy
was established in 1002, when he took Duke Richard's daughter,
Emma, as his second wife. In 1013 the Viking Sweyn Forkbeard
secured mastery over the whole of England, forcing Ethelred into
exile in Normandy until Sweyn's death (1014). His nickname is a
mistranslation of Unraed ('ill advised'), a pun on his given name,
Aethelred ('good counsel').

f

Ferdinand I (1793–1875)
Emperor of Austria (1835–48)

The son of Holy Roman Emperor Francis II, whom he succeeded as Emperor of Austria. When the revolutionary movement broke out in 1847–8, he agreed to the appointment of a responsible ministry, but after the October rising in Vienna he abdicated in favour of his nephew, Francis Joseph.

Ferdinand I (1861–1948)
King of Bulgaria (1908–18)

On the abdication of Prince Alexander of Bulgaria (1887), Ferdinand accepted the crown and in 1908 proclaimed Bulgaria independent, taking the title of king or tsar. He joined the Balkan League against Turkey (1912) but, on breaking the league, ended losing more than he had gained. In October 1915 he invaded Serbia. His armies routed, he abdicated in 1918, his son Boris III succeeding him.

Ferdinand I (1503–64)
Holy Roman Emperor (1558–64)

The younger brother of Emperor Charles V, whom he succeeded. He was recognized as ruler of the Habsburg possessions in Austria (1521), elected king of Bohemia (1526), and seized the crown of Hungary (1527). Left by Charles V to conduct the affairs of the empire, he was unable to prevent Suleyman the Magnificent from seizing much of Hungary. Imperial forces successfully ended the Turkish seige of Vienna in 1529, but Austrian lands were again threatened by the Turks in 1532 and 1541. Although Ferdinand supported the emperor in 1546–7 in his campaign to crush the

Protestant rebellion, he was chiefly responsible for the religious compromise at Augsburg in 1555 that brought the religious wars to an end.

> Let justice be done, though the world may perish.
>
> *Attrib*

Ferdinand II (1578–1637)
Holy Roman Emperor (1619–37)

The grandson of Ferdinand I. His attempts to extend the policy of 'one church, one king' throughout the empire set in motion the Thirty Years War (1618–48). Threatened on two fronts, by the election of Protestants Frederick V as king of Bohemia, and Bethlen Gabor as king of Hungary, he gathered a formidable pan-Catholic force to overrun the Palatinate, rout the Bohemian Protestants and force Gabor to renounce the throne of Hungary. The war continued with Gustavus Adolphus of Sweden as the Protestant champion. Although the Swedish army was defeated at Nördlingen in 1634, Ferdinand accepted the compromise peace of Prague (1634), which was primarily effected by his son, the future Ferdinand III.

Ferdinand III (1608–57)
Holy Roman Emperor (from 1637), King of Hungary (from 1625) and Bohemia (from 1627)

The son of Ferdinand II, whom he succeeded. As emperor, he continued the struggle against the Protestants but opened negotiations at Münster in 1644, and in 1648 signed the Peace of Westphalia that ended the Thirty Years War.

Ferdinand III (1200–52)
King of Castile (from 1217) and of Leon (from 1230)

From 1224 he devoted himself to the overthrow of the weakened Muslim dynasty of the Almohads, achieving a major breakthrough with the capture of Cordoba in 1236. By his death he had seized more Muslim territory that any other Spanish king, and reduced the remaining Muslim states to vassal kingdoms of Castile. He was canonized in 1671.

Ferdinand V, the Catholic (1452–1516)
King of Castile (1474–1504), of Aragon (as Ferdinand II, 1479–1516), of Sicily (1468–1516) and of Naples (1504–16)

The son of John II of Navarre and Aragon. Through his marriage (1469) to Isabella of Castile, he united the crowns of Aragon and Castile to form the basis of modern Spain. He campaigned vigorously against the Moors in Spain, and finally conquered Granada in 1492 — the same year in which he expelled the Jews from the kingdom and financed Columbus's expedition to the Americas. He earned his title 'the Catholic' for helping the pope drive the French from Naples (1503). On Isabella's death in 1504 he retained control of Castile by placing their insane daughter the Infanta Joanna on the throne, with himself as regent. He was succeeded by his grandson, the Holy Roman Emperor Charles.

Ferdinand VI (1711–59)
King of Spain (1746–59)

The son of Philip V, whom he succeeded. Following the disadvantageous treaty of Aix-la-Chapelle in 1747, he did his best to keep Spain neutral in European conflicts. He was succeeded by his half-brother, Charles III.

Ferdinand VII (1788–1833)
King of Spain (1808–33)

The eldest son of Charles IV, who abdicated in his favour when Napoleon invaded Spain in 1808. He spent six years in exile before being restored to the throne in 1813, whereupon he refused to accept the liberal Constitution of Cadiz (1812) and, although a revolution in 1820 forced him briefly to reinstate it, embarked upon a period of counter-revolutionary terror.

Ferdinand I (1751–1825)
King of the Two Sicilies (1816–25), and of Naples (as Ferdinand IV, 1759–99, 1799–1806)

He joined England and Austria against France (1793), but was forced to make a treaty with Napoleon (1801) and to flee to Sicily under English protection (1806). He was reinstated by the Congress of Vienna in 1815 and a year later united his two states in the Kingdom of the Two Sicilies.

Ferdinand II (1810–59)
King of the Two Sicilies (1830–59)

The son of Francis I, whom he succeeded. In 1848 he granted a constitution, but the Sicilians mistrusted his promises and declared that he had forfeited the crown. He subdued the revolt in Sicily by bombarding its chief cities, then set aside the constitution, and persecuted those who had taken part in reforms. He was succeeded by his son Francis II (1836–94), who fell in 1860–1 before Garibaldi and the attainment of Italian unity.

Francis I (1494–1547)
King of France (1515–47)

The nephew and son-in-law of Louis XII, whom he succeeded. He combined the qualities of the medieval knight and the Renaissance prince, though he became increasingly hostile to Protestantism after 1534. His reign was dominated by his rivalry with Emperor Charles V, which led to a series of wars (1521–6, 1528–9, 1536–8, 1542–4).

> He is a Frenchman and I cannot say how far you should trust him.
>   *Henry VIII*, Venetian Calendar

Francis II (1544–60)
King of France (1559–60)

The eldest son of Henry II and Catherine de' Medici. In 1558 he married Mary, Queen of Scots. His short reign was dominated by the Guise family, in their struggle against the Protestants.

Francis I (1708–65)
Holy Roman Emperor (1745–65)

The eldest son of Leopold, Duke of Lorraine and Grand Duke of Tuscany. In 1736 he married Maria Theresa of Austria.

Francis II (1768–1835)
Holy Roman Emperor (1792–1806), Emperor of Austria (as Francis I, 1804–35), King of Hungary and Bohemia (1792–1835)

The last Holy Roman Emperor, he succeeded his father Leopold II. Defeated on several occasions by Napoleon (1797, 1801, 1805,

1809), he made a short-lived alliance with him, marrying his daughter, Marie Louise, to the French Emperor. Later he joined with Russia and Prussia to win the battle of Leipzig (1813), and by the Treaty of Vienna (1815) he recovered Lombardy, Venetia and Galacia.

Francis Joseph or Franz Josef I (1830–1916)
Emperor of Austria (1848–1916) and King of Hungary (1867–1916)

The grandson of Emperor Francis I and nephew of Ferdinand I, whom he succeeded. During his reign the nationalistic hopes of the various groups within the empire were suppressed. He was defeated by the Prussians in 1866, and reorganized his empire into the dual monarchy of Austria–Hungary in 1867. His annexation of Bosnia-Herzegovina in 1908 shook Europe, and his attack on Serbia in 1914 (following the assassination of his nephew, Archduke Francis Ferdinand, by Serbian nationalists) triggered World War I.

Fredegond (d.597)
Frankish queen

The wife of Chilperic, King of Neustria. She waged a relentless feud with Brunhilde of Austrasia, a feud intensified by the rivalry between the two kingdoms.

Frederick I, Barbarossa (Redbeard) (c.1123–1190)
Holy Roman Emperor (1152–90)

The nephew of Conrad III, whom he succeeded. His reign was a continual struggle against unruly vassals at home, the city-republics of Lombardy, and the papacy. One of his campaigns in Italy resulted in the defeat of Legnano (1176), but he crushed Henry the Lion of Bavaria and asserted his feudal superiority over Poland, Hungary, Denmark and Burgandy. He led the Third Crusade against Saladin (1189) and was victorious at Philomelium and Iconium. He was succeeded by his son, Henry VI.

Frederick II (1194–1250)
Holy Roman Emperor (1220–50), King of Sicily (from 1198) and of Germany (from 1212)

The grandson of Frederick I and son of Henry VI, whom he succeeded. He aimed to increase Imperial power in Italy, but his plans were frustrated by the Lombard cities and by the popes. In 1228 he set out on the Fifth Crusade, took possession of Jersusalem, and crowned himself king there (1229).

Frederick III, of Germany (1415–93)
King of Germany (from 1440) and Holy Roman Emperor (1452–93)

Throughout his reign wars raged on the frontiers of the empire, and disorder raged within. He lost his hold upon Switzerland, Milan, Bohemia, and Hungary; and remained apathetic under two Turkish invasions (1469 and 1475). Nevertheless, by the marriage of his son, Maximilian I, to Mary, daughter of Charles the Bold of Burgundy, he laid the foundation of the future greatness of the Habsburgs.

Frederick V, the Winter King (1596–1632)
Elector of the Palatinate (1610–23) and King of Bohemia (as Frederick I, 1619–20)

He married Elizabeth, daughter of James I of England (1613), and as leader of the Protestant Union of Germany accepted the Crown of Bohemia (1619), which he held only for one winter before his defeat at White Mountain (1620) by Imperialist-Spanish forces.

Frederick I (1471–1533)
King of Denmark and Norway (1523–33)

The son of Christian I. He became king when his nephew, Christian II, was dethroned by a rebellion in Denmark. In 1531–2 he fended off an invasion of Norway by the ex-king; whom he captured by trickery and imprisoned. He was succeeded by his son Christian III.

Frederick II (1534–88)
King of Denmark (1559–88)

The son and successor of Christian III. After a seven-year war against Sweden, which ended inconclusively with the Treaty of Stettin (1370), the remainder of his reign was a period of peace and prosperity. He was succeeded by his son, Christian IV.

Frederick III (1609–70)
King of Denmark and Norway (1648–70)

The son and successor of Christian IV. The first half of his reign was taken up with costly wars against Sweden; but after the peace

settlement of 1660 he established hereditary monarchy over
Denmark, Norway and Iceland.

Frederick VI (1768–1839)
King of Denmark (1808–39) and Norway (1808–14)

The son of Christian VII, whom he succeeded. During his liberal
reign, serfdom was abolished, the criminal code amended, and the
slave trade outlawed in the Danish colonies. He refused to join Britain
against Napoleon, and after the war lost Norway to Sweden (1814).
In 1831 he granted a liberal constitution to his subjects.

Frederick VII (1808–63)
King of Denmark (1848–63)

The son and successor of Christian VIII. In 1849 he accepted a new
and liberal constitution abolishing absolute monarchy. He died
childless, and was succeeded by Christian IX.

Frederick VIII (1843–1912)
King of Denmark (1906–12)

The son and successor of Christian IX, and brother of Queen
Alexandra of Britain. In 1907 he made a state visit to Iceland to
celebrate the granting of home rule there (1904). His second son
became King Haakon VII of Norway. He was succeeded by his eldest
son, Christian X.

Frederick IX (1899–1972)
King of Denmark (1947–72)

The son of Christian X, whom he succeeded. In 1935 he married
Ingrid, daughter of Gustavus VI of Sweden. They had three daughters:
Margrethe (later Margrethe II), Benedikte, and Anne-Marie, who
married the former King Constantine II of Greece. During World
War II, he encouraged the Danish resistance movement, and was
imprisoned by the Germans (1943–5).

Frederick I (1657–1713)
King of Prussia (1701–1713)

He became elector of Brandenburg in 1688 (as Frederick III) and was
made the first king of Prussia in 1701 for his loyalty to Emperor
Leopold against the French. He established a standing army and was
a great patron of the arts and learning.

Frederick II, the Great (1712–86)
King of Prussia (1740–86)

The son of Frederick-William I, whom he succeeded. He was a noted
military commander in the War of the Austrian Succession (1740–
8). He seized Silesia, and defeated the Austrians at Mollwitz (1741)
and Chotusitz (1742). The second Silesian War (1744–5) left him
with further territories, which he retained after fighting the Seven
Years War (1756–63). In 1772 he shared in the first partition of
Poland. Under him, Prussia doubled in area, strengthened its economy
and became a leading European power.

> My people and I have come to an agreement which satisfies us both.
> They are to say what they please, and I am to do what I please.
>
> *Attrib, on benevolent despotism*

Frederick III (1831–88)
German Emperor and King of Prussia (1888)

The only son of William I, whom he succeeded. Crown prince of
Prussia (from 1861) and of the German Empire (from 1871), he had
a great horror of war, detested autocratic ideas, and tried to liberalize
German institutions. He died shortly after being proclaimed emperor
and was succeeded by his son, William II.

Frederick I (1675–1751)
King of Sweden (1720–51)

In 1715 he married Ulrika Eleonora, the sister of King Charles XII
and future queen of Sweden. In 1720 his wife abdicated the throne
in his favour, under a new constitution which deprived the crown of
most of its authority. He died childless, and was succeeded by Adolf
Frederick.

Frederick-William I (1688–1740)
King of Prussia (1713–40)

The son of Frederick I, whom he succeeded. He encouraged native
industries, swept away the last traces of the feudal system and followed
a policy of religious toleration. By establishing a centralized
administrative system and a formidable army, he laid the foundation

of the future power of Prussia. He was succeeded by his son, Frederick the Great.

> The soul is God's. Everything else is mine.
>
> *One of his absolutist principles*

Frederick-William II (1744–97)
King of Prussia (1786–97)

The nephew of Frederick II, the Great, whom he succeeded. He became increasingly unpopular as a result of his dependence on favourites, his denial of press and religious freedoms, his weak foreign policy and the debt and heavy taxation with which he oppressed his subjects. He acquired large areas of Polish Prussia and Silesia by the partitions of Poland in 1793 and 1795.

Frederick-William III (1770–1840)
King of Prussia (1797–1840)

The son of Frederick-William II, whom he succeeded. Though at first neutral towards Napoleon's conquests, he declared war in 1806, was severely defeated at Jena and Auerstadt, and lost all territory west of the Elbe (1807). Following a reorganization of both government and army, he shared in the victory of Leipzig (1813). By the Treaty of Vienna (1815) he recovered his lands, and thereafter tended to support the forces of conservatism.

Frederick-William IV (1795–1861)
King of Prussia (1840–61)

The son of Frederick-William III, whom he succeeded. He began his reign with minor reforms and promises of radical change, but opposed the popular movement of 1848 until he was forced by an uprising to grant a representative parliament in 1850. His brother (later William I) was regent from 1858.

g

Gaiseric or Genseric (c.390–477 AD)
King of the Vandals and Alans (AD 428–77)

He led the Vandals in their invasion of Gaul, then crossed from Spain to Numidia (AD 429), captured and sacked Hippo (AD 430), seized Carthage (AD 439), and made it his capital. He built up a large sea power in the western Mediterranean, and in AD 455 he sacked Rome. He was succeeded by his son Huneric.

George I (1660–1727)
King of Great Britain and Ireland (1714–27)

The great-grandson of James I of England. Elector of Hanover since 1698, he had commanded the Imperial forces in the Marlborough wars, and was proclaimed king on the death of Queen Anne. He divorced his wife and cousin, Princess Dorothea of Zell, imprisoning her in the castle of Ahlde, where she died (1726). He took relatively little part in the government of Britain, for his affections remained with Hanover, where he spent much of his life.

George II (1683–1760)
King of Great Britain and Ireland, and Elector of Hanover (1727–60)

The son of George I, whom he succeeded. He married Caroline of Ansbach in 1705, and his government policy was formulated at first by Robert Walpole. George fought in the War of the Austrian Succession, and the battle of Dettingen (1743) was the last time that a British monarch commanded an army in the field. His reign also saw the crushing of Jacobite hopes at the battle of Culloden (1746), the beginning of the Seven Years War (1756), the foundation of British India after the battle of Plassey (1757), and the capture of Quebec (1759).

George III (1738–1820)
King of Great Britain and Ireland (1760–1820), Elector (1760–1815) and King (1815–20) of Hanover

The grandson of George II, whom he succeeded. His eagerness to govern caused friction, and he was particularly unpopular in the 1770s when with Lord North he was blamed for the loss of the American colonies. In 1783 he called Pitt (the Younger) to office, thus ending the supremacy of the old Whig families. In 1810 his insanity increased, and his son George, Prince of Wales, was made regent.

> An old, mad, blind, despised and dying king.
>
> *Shelley, 'Sonnet: England in 1819'*

George IV (1762–1830)
King of Great Britain and Ireland and of Hanover (1820–30)

The eldest son of George III and prince regent from 1810, due to his father's insanity. His marriage to Mrs Fitzherbert, a Roman Catholic, was not acceptable in English law and in 1795 he married Princess Caroline of Brunswick, whom he tried unsuccessfully to divorce when he became king, causing considerable scandal. He was a patron of the arts and encouraged John Nash, who designed the Royal Pavilion in Brighton.

> Between the King and his brothers, the Government of this country is become a most heart-breaking concern. Nobody ever knew where he stands upon any subject.
>
> *1828 Duke of Wellington to Robert Peel, 26 Aug*

George V (1865–1936)
King of Great Britain and Northern Ireland (1910–36)

The second son of Edward VII. In 1893 he married Princess Mary of Teck. He served in the navy, travelled in many parts of the empire, and was created Prince of Wales in 1901. His reign saw the Union of South Africa (1910), World War I (1914–18), the Irish Free State settlement (1922), and the General Strike (1926).

> For seventeen years he did nothing at all but kill animals and stick in stamps.
>
> *1949 Sir Harold Nicholson*

George VI (1895–1952)
King of the United Kingdom (1936–52)

The second son of George V. He served in the Grand Fleet at the
battle of Jutland (1916), was created Duke of York in 1920, and
married in 1923. He came to the throne on the abdication of his elder
brother, Edward VIII. During World War II he continued to reside
in bomb-damaged Buckingham Palace, visited all theatres of war, and
delivered many broadcasts, overcoming his speech impediment. His
wife Elizabeth, born Elizabeth Angela Marguerite Bowes-Lyon
(1900–), also paid many wartime visits. They had two children:
Princess Elizabeth (later Queen Elizabeth II) and Princess Margaret.

George I (1845–1913)
King of Greece (1863–1913)

The second son of King Christian IX of Denmark. He was elected
king by the Greek national assembly on the deposition of King Otto
of Greece. Involved in the Balkan War of 1912–13, he was assassinated
at Salonika, and succeeded by his son, Constantine I.

George II (1890–1947)
King of Greece (1922–3, 1935–47)

The son of Constantine I, he succeeded to the throne on his father's
second abdication in 1922, but was deposed in 1923 by a military
junta. Restored to the throne in 1935, he declared a dictatorship
under Yanni Metaxas. When Greece was overrun by the Germans in
World War II, he fled to Crete and then England, returning in 1946.
He was succeeded by his brother Paul I.

George V (1819–78)
King of Hanover (1851–66)

Blind from 1833 and a complete absolutist, in that he had an
exaggerated sense of the importance of the house of Welf and was
constantly disputing with the diet. He lost Hanover to Prussia as a
result of refusing to remain neutral in the Austro-Prussian war of
1866. He died an exile in Paris.

Gloucester, Humphrey, Duke of (1391–1447)
Lord Protector during the minority of Henry VI (1422–9)

The youngest son of Henry IV. He increased the difficulties of his brother, the Duke of Bedford, by his greed, irresponsibility, and quarrels with their uncle, Cardinal Beaufort. In 1447 he was arrested for high treason and five days later died (apparently from natural causes).

Grey, Lady Jane (1537–54)
Queen of England for nine days in 1553

The great-granddaughter of Henry VII and eldest daughter of Henry Grey, Marquis of Dorset. In 1553 the Duke of Northumberland, who wanted to ensure that a Protestant would succeed the dying Edward VI, married Jane (against her wish) to his fourth son, Lord Guildford Dudley. Declared queen three days after Edward's death (9 Jul), she was soon forced to abdicate in favour of Mary, and imprisoned. Following a rebellion in her favour, she was beheaded.

Guise, Mary of or Mary of Lorraine (1515–60)
Wife of James V of Scotland

The daughter of Claude of Lorraine, first Duke of Guise. In 1538 she married James V of Scotland, at whose death (1542) she was left with one child, Mary, Queen of Scots. As queen regent (from 1554) she allowed the Guises so much influence that the Protestant nobles raised a rebellion (1559), which continued until her death in Edinburgh Castle.

Gundicarius or Gunther (c.385–437)
King of the Burgundians

The first recorded king of the Burgundians, he is said to have crossed the middle Rhine and established a new kingdom with his capital in the region of Worms. He was an ally of the Romans, but was killed when his army was routed by the Huns.

Gustavus I or Gustav Vasa (1496–1560)
King of Sweden (1523–60)

In 1518 he was taken to Denmark as a hostage, but he escaped and led a peasant rising against the occupying Danes. He captured Stockholm, drove the enemy from Sweden and was elected king. Despite several rebellions, his 40-year reign left Sweden peaceful.

Gustavus II or **Gustavus Adolphus** (1594–1632)
King of Sweden (1611–32)

The son of Charles IX, whom he succeeded. He reorganized the government and recovered his Baltic provinces from Denmark. He ended wars with Russia (1617) and Poland (1629), and carried out major military and economic reforms at home. In 1630 he entered the Thirty Years War, leading the German Protestants against the Imperialist forces, and won several victories, notably at Breitenfeld (1631), and at Lützen, where he was killed.

Gustavus III (1746–92)
King of Sweden (1771–92)

The son and successor of King Adolf Frederick. He declared a new form of government (1772), and granted religious toleration, but also created a secret police system and introduced censorship. From 1788 to 1790 he waged an unpopular and inconclusive war against Russia, assuming new royal powers as an absolute monarch in 1789. Following the outbreak of the French Revolution, he planned to use his army to assist Louis XVI, but in March 1792 he was assassinated. He was succeeded by his son, Gustavus IV Adolf.

Gustavus IV Adolf (1778–1837)
King of Sweden (1792–1809)

The son and successor of Gustavus III. In 1805 he abandoned Swedish neutrality and declared war on France — a decision that cost him Swedish Pomerania and Finland. He was overthrown by a military coup in 1809 and was succeeded by his uncle, Charles XIII, under a new constitution that limited the absolute power of the monarchy.

Gustavus V (1858–1950)
King of Sweden (1907–50)

The son of Oskar II, whom he succeeded. In his famous 'Courtyard Speech' (1914), he challenged the government with a call for greater spending on defence. Demands for his abdication were stilled by the outbreak of World War I, when Sweden mobilized but remained neutral. Thereafter he reigned as a popular constitutional monarch. He was succeeded by his son, Gustavus VI.

Gustavus VI (1882–1973)
King of Sweden (1950–73)

The son and successor of Gustavus V. He was a respected scholar and archaeologist. In 1905 he married Princess Margaret (1882–1920), a grand-daughter of Queen Victoria, by whom he had four sons and a daughter; and in 1923 he married Lady Louise Mountbatten (1889–1965), sister of Earl Mountbatten of Burma. During his reign he worked to transform the crown into a democratic monarchy, which helped to preserve it against political demands for a republic. He was succeeded by his grandson, Carl XVI Gustaf.

Guthorm or Guthrum (d.890)
Danish king of East Anglia

He led a major Viking invasion of Anglo-Saxon England in 871, seized East Anglia and conquered Northumbria and Mercia. His attack on Wessex ended in defeat at the battle of Edington in Wiltshire (878), whereupon he accepted baptism as a Christian, and settled down peacefully, with his army, in East Anglia.

h

Haakon I, the Good (914–61)
King of Norway (c.945–61)

The youngest son of Harold I, he was brought up in England at the Christian court of King Athelstan. When news came of his father's death, he returned to Norway, where he seized the throne from his half-brother, Erik Blood-axe, and attempted unsuccessfully to convert Norway to Christianity. He died in battle against the sons of Erik Blood-axe.

Haakon IV, the Old (1204–63)
King of Norway (1217–63)

He annexed Greenland (1261) and Iceland (1262), and in 1263 tried to claim Norway's traditional rights over the Hebrides. He died in Orkney, after his defeat at Largs by Alexander III of Scotland.

Haakon VII (1872–1957)
King of Norway (1905–57)

He became king when Norway voted for independence from Sweden in 1905. Known as 'the People's King', after the German invasion of Norway (1940) he continued his resistance to Nazi occupation from England, returning in triumph in 1945.

Hardicanute or Harthacnut (c.1018–42)
King of Denmark (1035–42), and of England (1040–2)

King Canute had intended that Hardicanute, his only son by Emma of Normandy, should succeed him in both Denmark and England. However, Hardicanute was unable to inherit the English throne until his stepbrother, Harold I, died (1040). He himself died childless, and was succeeded by his half-brother Edward the Confessor, the son of Emma and Ethelred the Unready.

Harold I, Harefoot (c.1016–40)
King of England (1037–40)

The younger son of Canute and Aelfgifu of Northampton. Canute
had intended that Hardicanute, his only son by Emma of Normandy,
and the half-brother of Harold, should succeed him in both Denmark
and England, but due to Hardicanute's absence in Denmark, Harold
was accepted in England, first as regent (1035–6), and from 1037 as
king.

Harold II (c.1022–66)
King of England (1066)

The second son of Earl Godwin and last Anglo-Saxon king of England.
He was created Earl of East Anglia (1045); succeeded to his father's
earldom of Wessex (1053); and on the death of Edward the Confessor
(Jan 1066) was crowned king. He defeated his brother Tostig and
Harold III of Norway at Stamford Bridge (Sep 1066), but Duke
William of Normandy then invaded England, and defeated and killed
Harold near Hastings (14 Oct 1066).

Harold, Blue-tooth (c.910–85)
King of Denmark (c.950–85)

The son of Gorm the Old, he was the first king to unify all the
provinces of Denmark under a single crown. He was converted to
Christianity in c.960, made Christianity the state religion of Denmark,
and repelled attacks from Norway and Germany. He was deposed by
his son Sweyn Forkbeard.

Harold I, Fine-hair (c.865–945)
King of Norway (c.890–942)

The son of Halfdan the Black (King of Vestfold). He was the first
ruler to claim sovereignty over all Norway, defeating his opponents
at the naval battle of Hafursfjord, off Stavanger. His authoritarian rule
caused many to emigrate west to the Orkneys, Hebrides, Ireland,
and Iceland. He made several expeditions across the North Sea to
impose Norwegian rule over the Northern and Western Isles of
Scotland. He abdicated in favour of his eldest son, Erik Blood-axe.

Harold II, Greycloak (d.970)
King of Norway (c.965–70)

The eldest son of Erik Blood-axe. With Danish support he and his four brothers made several assaults on Norway from 960 onwards and eventually defeated and killed King Haakon I in battle off Hardangerfjord. However, when Greycloak tried to break free of his alliance with Denmark, Earl Haakon of Lade, enlisted Danish help for another invasion, and Greycloak was captured and killed.

Harold III, Hardrada (the Ruthless) (1015–66)
King of Norway (1047–66)

Until 1045 he served in Constantinople as captain of the Scandinavian bodyguard of the Greek emperors. On his return to Norway, he divided the kingdom with his nephew Magnus, and then became sole ruler (1047). In 1066 he landed in England to support Tostig against the English King Harold II, but was killed at the Battle of Stamford Bridge.

Henrietta Maria (1609–69)
Queen-consort of Charles I of England

The youngest child of Henry IV of France. She married Charles in 1625, but her French attendants and Catholic religion made her unpopular. In 1642 she fled to Holland to raise funds for the Royalist cause, returning a year later to meet Charles near Edgehill. In 1644, shortly after giving birth to Henrietta Anne, she fled to France. She paid two visits to England after the Restoration (1660–1, 1662–5).

Henry I (1068–1135)
King of England (from 1100) and Duke of Normandy (from 1106)

The youngest son of William the Conqueror and brother of William II, whom he succeeded. He conquered Normandy from his brother, Robert Curthose, at the battle of Tinchebrai (1106), and ruled both his domains with the aim of financing warfare and alliances. In 1127 he chose as his heir his daughter Empress Matilda, widow of Emperor Henry V of Germany (and from 1128 wife of Geoffrey Plantagenet, Count of Anjou), but after his death the Crown was seized by his nephew Stephen.

Henry II (1133–89)
King of England (1154–89)

The son of Geoffrey Plantagenet, Count of Anjou, and Empress Matilda — Henry I's daughter and acknowledged heir. He became Duke of Normandy (1150), Count of Anjou (1151), and, through his marriage to Eleanor of Aquitaine (1152), Duke of Aquitaine. In 1153 he invaded England to succeed Stephen, founding the Plantagenet dynasty of English kings. He restored royal control over the barons, but his efforts to limit the power of the Church caused conflict with his former chancellor, Thomas Becket, Archbishop of Canterbury, which ended only with Becket's murder (1170). He led a major expedition to Ireland (1171), which resulted in its annexation. He faced two rebellions from his family, the first in 1173–4 , and the second in 1189, when his sons John and Richard allied with Philip II of France and overran Maine and Touraine. Henry agreed a peace which recognized Richard as his sole heir for all his domains, which stretched from the Scottish borders to the Pyrenees.

> The king sought to help those of his subjects who could least help themselves.
>
> *Ralph Diceto, a canon of St Paul's Cathedral*

Henry III (1207–72)
King of England (1216–72)

The elder son and successor of John. He declared an end to his minority in 1227, and asserted his royal rights in a way that annoyed the barons and conflicted with the principles of Magna Carta. Led by the King's brother-in-law, Simon de Montfort, the barons imposed the Provisions of Oxford (1258), which gave them a definite say in government. On his attempt to restore royal power, they rebelled and captured the King at Lewes (1264), but were defeated at Evesham (1265). The Dictum of Kenilworth (1266), though favourable to Henry, urged him to observe Magna Carta. He was succeeded by his son, Edward I.

Henry IV, Bolingbroke (1366–1413)
King of England (1399–1413)

The first king of England from the House of Lancaster. The son of

John of Gaunt, and grandson of Edward III. In 1397 he supported
Richard II against the Duke of Gloucester. Banished in 1398, the
following year Henry persuaded Richard to abdicate in his favour.
His reign featured rebellion and lawlessness, and he was constantly
hampered by lack of money. Under Owen Glendower the Welsh
kept their independence, and Henry was defeated when he attacked
Scotland (1400). Henry Percy (Hotspur) and his house then joined
with the Scots and the Welsh against him, but they were defeated at
Shrewsbury (1403).

Henry V (1387–1422)
King of England (1413–22)

The eldest son of Henry IV. He fought against Glendower and the
Welsh rebels (1402–8), and became constable of Dover (1409) and
captain of Calais (1410). His reign was marked by his claim, through
his great-grandfather Edward III, to the French Crown. In 1415 he
invaded France, won the battle of Agincourt against great odds, and
by 1419 Normandy was under English control. By the 'perpetual
peace' of Troyes (1420), Henry was recognized as heir to the French
throne and Regent of France, and married to Charles VI's daughter,
Catherine of Valois. Only 15 months after their marriage, however,
Henry died suddenly.

Henry VI (1421–71)
King of England (1422–61, 1470–1)

The only child of Henry V and Catherine of Valois. During his
minority, his uncle Humphrey, Duke of Gloucester, was Lord
Protector of England, and another uncle, John, Duke of Bedford, was
Regent in France. However, the French territories were gradually
lost and by 1453 the English held only Calais. When Henry began to
suffer from bouts of insanity, Richard, Duke of York, seized power
as Lord Protector (1454) and defeated the king's army at St Albans
(1455). York himself was killed at Wakefield (1460), but his heir was
proclaimed king as Edward IV after Henry's deposition (1461). In
1464 Henry returned from exile in Scotland to lead the Lancastrian
cause, but was captured and imprisoned (1465–70). Richard Neville,
Earl of Warwick, restored him to the throne (Oct 1470), but his
nominal rule ended on Edward IV's return to London (Apr 1471).

After the Yorkist victory at Tewkesbury (May 1471), Henry was murdered in the Tower.

> The realm of England was out of all good governance, as it had been many days before, for the king was simple and led by covetous counsel.
>
> *Anonymous chronicler*

Henry VII (1457–1509)
King of England (1485–1509)

The first Tudor king of England, the grandson of Owen Tudor and Catherine of Valois (widow of Henry V). After the Lancastrian defeat at Tewkesbury (1471), Henry was taken to Brittany. He returned to England in 1485 and defeated Richard III at Bosworth. As king, his policy was to restore peace and prosperity to the country, which was helped by his marriage of reconciliation with Elizabeth of York, but he dealt firmly with Yorkist plots (eg the one led by Perkin Warbeck). Peace was concluded with France, and the marriage of his heir (Henry VIII) to Catherine of Aragon cemented an alliance with Spain.

> A dark prince and infinitely suspicious, and his time full of secret conspiracies.
>
> *1621 Sir Francis Bacon, Life of Henry VII*

Henry VIII (1491–1547)
King of England (1509–47)

The second son of Henry VII, whom he succeeded. He married his brother Arthur's widow, Catherine of Aragon (1509). As a member of the Holy League, he invaded France (1512) and won the battle of The Spurs (1513), while during his absence the Scots were defeated at Flodden. At this time Thomas Wolsey rose to prominence as his advisor. In 1521 Henry received from the pope the title 'Defender of the Faith', but when in 1527 he decided to divorce Catherine the pope failed to grant his wish and Wolsey fell from favour. In defiance of Rome Henry was privately married to Anne Boleyn (1533) and in 1534 it was enacted that his marriage to Catherine was invalid, and that the king was the sole head of the Church of England. The policy of suppressing the monasteries, begun under Wolsey, continued in earnest under Thomas Cromwell. Anne Boleyn was executed for infidelity (1836). Henry then married: Jane Seymour, who died (1537) leaving a son (later Edward VI); Anne of Cleves (1540), whom

he soon divorced; Catherine Howard (1540), who was executed on
a charge of infidelity (1542); and Catherine Parr (1543), who survived
him. In his later years he warred again with France and Scotland,
before peace was concluded with France (1546). His reign saw a
complete break with the Roman Catholic church, as well as the
legalized murder of those like Sir Thomas More, who dared to oppose
his will.

> The King was so fat that three of the biggest men that could be
> found could get inside his doublet.
>
> *c.1550* The Spanish Chronicle

Henry I (1008–60)
King of France (1031–60)

The son and successor of Robert II. He was involved in struggles with
William, Duke of Normandy, and with Burgundy, which he had
unwisely granted to his rival brother, Robert.

Henry II (1519–59)
King of France (1547–59)

The second son of Francis I and first husband (1533) of Catherine de'
Medici. Soon after he came to the throne, he began to oppress his
Protestant subjects. Through the influence of the Guises he formed
an alliance with Scotland, and declared war against England, which
ended in 1558 with his taking Calais. He continued the long-standing
war against the emperor Charles V, gaining Toul, Metz, and Verdun,
but suffered losses in Italy and the Low Countries, which led to the
Treaty of Cateau-Cambrésis (1559).

Henry III (1551–89)
King of France (1574–89) and of Poland (1573–5)

The third son of Henry II and brother of Charles IX, whom he
succeeded. He gained victories over the Huguenots (1569), and was
active in the St Bartholomew's Day Massacre (1572). His reign was
marked throughout by civil war between Huguenots and Catholics.
In 1588 he arranged the assassination of the Duke of Guise, which
enraged the Catholic League. He then joined forces with his brother-
in-law, the Huguenot Henry of Navarre, who succeeded him on his
assassination.

Henry IV or Henry of Navarre (1553–1610)
King of France (1589–1610)

The son of Antoine de Bourbon and Jeanne d'Albret. He led the Huguenot army at the battle of Jarnac (1569), and became leader of the Protestant Party. After the St Bartholomew's Day Massacre (1572), he spent three years virtually a prisoner at the French court, but escaped in 1576 and resumed command of the army in continuing opposition to the Catholic League. He succeeded to the throne after the murder of Henry III, and in 1593 became a Catholic — although by the Edict of Nantes Protestants were allowed to practise their religion. His economic policies gradually brought new wealth to the country. He was assassinated by a religious fanatic.

> I want there to be no peasant in my kingdom so poor that he is unable to have a chicken in his pot every Sunday.
>
> *Attrib*

Henry I, the Fowler (c.876–936)
King of Germany (919–36)

He brought Swabia and Bavaria into the German confederation, regained Lotharingia (925), defeated the Wends (928) and the Hungarians (933) and seized Schleswig from Denmark (934). He was about to claim the imperial crown as Holy Roman Emperor in 936 when he died. He was succeeded by his son, Otto the Great.

Henry III (1017–56)
Holy Roman Emperor (1039–56) and King of the Germans (1026–56)

The son of Conrad II, whom he succeeded. He became king of the Germans (1026), Duke of Bavaria (1027), Duke of Swabia (1038) and as emperor stretched the boundaries of his rule over Bohemia, Hungary, Apulia and Calabria. In 1046 he deposed all three rival popes, electing Clement II in their place.

Henry IV (1050–1106)
Holy Roman Emperor (1056–1105) and King of the Germans (1053–1105)

The son of Henry III, whom he succeeded. The great duel between Pope Gregory VII and the emperor began in 1076 with Henry declaring the pope deposed. Gregory responded by excommunicating

Henry, and although the emperor submitted, he soon renewed the conflict and was again excommunicated. He thereupon appointed a new pope, Clement III, besieged Rome, and in 1084 was crowned by the antipope. He returned to Germany to stamp out the civil war there, but in 1090 his son Conrad joined his enemies and in 1105 his second son (later Emperor Henry V) deposed him.

Henry VI (1165–97)
Holy Roman Emperor (from 1191), King of Germany (from 1190) and of Sicily (from 1194)

The son and successor of Frederick I Barbarossa and husband (from 1186) of Constance, heiress of William II of Sicily. He was opposed by the pope, the Guelfs, Richard I of England and Constance's illegitimate brother Tancred who had been elected king of Sicily on the death of William This hostile alliance collapsed when Richard became Henry's captive, and on Tancred's death (1194) Henry overran Sicily. Regarded by contemporaries as the most powerful man on earth, he died while still young and was succeeded by his son, Frederick II.

Henry VII (1274–1313)
Holy Roman Emperor and King of Germany (1308–13)

Originally Count of Luxembourg, he was elected emperor as an alternative candidate to Charles of Valois. In 1310 he marched on Italy with the aim of restoring his authority, but the imperialist cause collapsed when he died near Siena, probably of malaria.

Hiero I (d.c.467 BC)
King of Syracuse

He won a great naval victory over the Etruscans in 474 BC. Though reputedly violent and grasping, he had a keen interest in poetry, and was the patron of Simonides of Ceos, Aeschylus, Bacchylides, and Pindar.

Hiero II (3c BC)
King of Syracuse

He joined the Carthaginians in besieging Messana, which had surrendered to the Romans; but was defeated by Appius Claudius. In 258 BC he agreed a permanent peace with Rome and in the second Punic War he supported the Romans with money and troops.

Howard, Catherine (d.1542)
Queen-consort, the fifth wife of Henry VIII of England

A grand-daughter of the 2nd Duke of Norfolk. She became queen in the same month as Anne of Cleves was divorced (Jul 1540). A year later she was beheaded for treason, on a charge of infidelity.

Í

Ida (d.599)
King of Bernicia (Northumbria)

He was an Anglo-Saxon king who came northward over the river Tees, landing at Flamborough in 547. He established a fortified stronghold on the rock of Bamburgh as the capital of his new kingdom.

Isabella I, the Catholic (1451–1504)
Queen of Castile and Leon (from 1474) and of Aragon (from 1479)

The daughter of John II, King of Castile and Leon. In 1469 she married Ferdinand the Catholic of Aragon, with whom she ruled jointly from 1479. During her reign, the Inquisition was introduced (1478), the reconquest of Granada completed (1482–92), and the Jews expelled (1492), and she financed the voyage of Christopher Columbus to the New World.

Isabella II (1830–1904)
Queen of Spain (1833–68)

The daughter of Ferdinand VII, whom she succeeded. In 1846 she married her cousin, Francisco de Assisi. Although popular with the Spanish people, her scandalous private life made her the tool of rival factions and in 1868 she was deposed. She was succeeded by her son, Alfonso XII.

Isabella of Angoulême (d.1246)
Queen-consort of King John of England

She married John in 1200, and in 1214 was imprisoned by him at Gloucester. After his death in 1216 she returned to France. She was the mother of Henry III; her daughter, Isabella (1214–41), married the emperor Frederick II.

Isabella of France (1292–1358)
Queen-consort of Edward II of England

The daughter of Philip IV of France. In 1308 she married Edward II of England but then became the mistress of Roger Mortimer, with whom she overthrew and murdered the king (1327). Her son, Edward III, had Mortimer executed in 1330, and Isabella was sent into retirement.

Ivan III, the Great (1440–1505)
Grand Prince of Moscow (1462–1505)

He ended the Tartar overlordship of Moscow and gained control over several Russian principalities. In 1472 he assumed the title of 'Sovereign of all Russia' and adopted the emblem of the two-headed eagle of the Byzantine Empire.

Ivan IV, the Terrible (1530–84)
Tsar of Russia (1533–84)

The grandson of Ivan the Great. He subdued Kazan and Astrakhan, made the first inroads into Siberia, and established commercial links with England. In 1564, following the treachery of one of his counsellors, he embarked on a reign of terror, directed mainly at the feudal aristocracy (princes and boyars), but he nonetheless encouraged Russian culture and commerce. In 1581 he accidentally killed his eldest son, so that the throne passed on his death to his sickly second son, Theodore.

j

James I (1566–1625)
King of England (1603–25) and of Scotland (as James VI, 1567–1625)

The son of Mary, Queen of Scots, and Henry, Lord Darnley. On his mother's forced abdication, he was proclaimed king, and brought up by several regents. At first he ruled through his favourites, which caused a rebellion and a period of imprisonment. He hated Puritanism, and in 1600 managed to establish bishops in Scotland. As great-grandson of Margaret (daughter of Henry VII), he inherited the English throne on the death of Elizabeth I. He was himself succeeded by his son, Charles I.

> The wisest fool in Christendom.
>
> *Attrib Henri IV of France*

James II (1633–1701)
King of England and Ireland (1685–8) and of Scotland (as James VII)

The second son of Charles I and brother of Charles II, whom he succeeded. Nine months before his father's execution he escaped to Holland. At the Restoration (1660) he was made Lord High Admiral, and commanded the fleet in the Dutch Wars, but when he converted to Catholicism he was forced to resign his post. The 'Popish Plot' scare of 1678 forced him into exile, but attempts to exclude him from the succession failed and on Charles's death he succeeded to the throne. However his open support of Catholicism caused outrage, leading to the Glorious Revolution (1688), in which he was replaced by his son-in-law and nephew, William, Prince of Orange. His

attempt to regain his throne in Ireland ended in defeat at the battle
of the Boyne (1690).

> Kings being accountable for none of their actions but to God and
> themselves, ought to be more cautious and circumspect than those
> who are in lower stations.
>
> *James II in papers of advice drawn up for his son*

James I (1394–1437)
King of Scots (1406–37)

The third son of Robert III. He was sent for safety to France, but was
captured at sea (1406) and imprisoned in England, unable to rule
until his release in 1424. An accomplished poet, he wrote *The Kingis
Quair* to celebrate his romance with Joan Beaufort, a cousin of Henry V of
England. His ruthlessness towards the Stuarts led to his murder at Perth.

James II (1430–60)
King of Scots (1437–60)

The son of James I, whom he succeeded. He took control of the
government in 1449, and during the early years tried to reduce the
power of the mighty Black Douglases, whom he eventually defeated
in 1455 at Arkinholm, Dumfriesshire. He was killed during an attempt
to recapture Roxburgh Castle from the English.

James III (1452–88)
King of Scots (1460–88)

The eldest son of James II, whom he succeeded. He took control of
the government in 1469, the year of his marriage to Margaret of
Denmark, which brought Orkney and Shetland within the Scottish
realm (1472). He was defeated and killed by rebel nobles at the Battle
of Sauchieburn, near Stirling.

James IV (1473–1513)
King of Scots (1488–1513)

The eldest son of James III, whom he succeeded. In 1503 he married
Margaret Tudor, the eldest daughter of Henry VII — an alliance
which led ultimately to the union of the crowns in 1603. He
nevertheless renewed the French alliance when Henry VIII joined the
League against France, but his invasion of England resulted in his
defeat and death at the battle of Flodden, Northumberland.

James V (1512–42)
King of Scots (1513–42)

His father, James IV, died when he was an infant, leaving him to
grow up among the quarrelling pro-French and pro-English factions
in his country. In 1536 he visited France, and married first
Magdeleine, the daughter of Francis I (1537), and, after her death,
Mary of Guise (1538). In 1542 he warred with England, and an
attempted invasion ended in defeat at Solway Moss. He retired to
Falkland Palace where his daughter Mary (later Mary, Queen of Scots)
was born shortly before his death.

Jeanne d'Albret (1528–72)
Queen of Navarre

A Huguenot and a poet, she was the only daughter of Margaret of
Angoulême and Henry d'Albret of Navarre, whom she succeeded.
She married Antoine de Bourbon, Duc de Vendôme, in 1548, and
gave birth to the future Henry IV of France in 1553.

Joan, or Joanna, of Navarre (c.1370–1437)
Queen-consort of Henry IV of England

The widow of the Duke of Brittany, she married Henry IV in 1402.
After Henry's death in 1413, she was imprisoned for three years on
a charge of witchcraft.

Joan, or Joanna, the Mad (1479–1555)
Queen of Castile

The daughter of Ferdinand and Isabella of Spain. She married Philip
the Handsome of Flanders in 1495. On her mother's death in 1505,
she became queen of Castile. Philip died the same year and Joan
(Juana), who suffered from severe melancholia, was imprisoned while
her father assumed the regency of Castile. Although Ferdinand died
in 1516, her son Charles, King of Spain, kept her a prisoner until her
death.

Johan III (1537–92)
King of Sweden (1568–92)

The son of King Gustavus I. With his younger brother (the future
Charles IX), he deposed his half-brother Erik XIV in 1568. He brought
the seven-year war with Denmark to a close with the Treaty of Stettin

(1570); and in 1578–83 joined with Poland in a war against Russia. He married Katarina Jagellonica, sister of Sigismund II Augustus of Poland, and had their Catholic son Sigismund III Vasa crowned king of Poland in 1587. He was succeeded on the Swedish throne by Sigismund III of Poland, who was soon deposed, however, and succeeded by Charles IX.

John (1167–1216)
King of England (1199–1216)

The youngest son of Henry II. Although he tried to seize the Crown during Richard I's captivity in Germany (1193–4), Richard nevertheless chose him as his successor, despite the superior claim of Arthur, the son of John's elder brother Geoffrey. Arthur's claims were supported by Philip II of France, and after Arthur's murder (1203), Philip seized most of Aquitaine. As a result of John's refusal to accept Stephen Langton as Archbishop of Canterbury he was excommunicated (1209–13). His oppressive government, and failure to recover Normandy, drove the barons to demand constitutional reform. In 1215 they forced him to accept the Great Charter (Magna Carta), the basis of the English constitution, which he later rejected, triggering the first Barons War (1215–17)

John, the Blind (1296–1346)
King of Bohemia (1311–46)

The son of Count Henry III of Luxembourg (later Emperor Henry VII). Having married (1310) Elizabeth, the heiress of Bohemia, he was crowned king in 1311. He contributed to the Bavarian victory at Mühldorf in 1322, and in 1346 (by which time he was completely blind) he fell at the battle of Crécy, fighting on the side of the French.

John II, the Good (1319–64)
King of France (1350–64)

The son of Philip VI. He was captured by Edward the Black Prince at the battle of Poitiers (1356), and taken to England, but returned home after the treaty of Brétigny (1360), leaving his second son, the Duke of Anjou, as a hostage. When the duke escaped (1363), John chivalrously returned to London, and died there.

John I or **John Zápolya** (1487–1540)
King of Hungary (1526–40)

A Transylvanian prince. He was proclaimed king despite the superior
Habsburg claim of Emperor Ferdinand I, who drove him out in 1527.
He was reinstated as a puppet ruler by Suleyman the Magnificent.

John II or **John Sigismund Zápolya** (1540–71)
King of Hungary (1540–1)

The son of John Zápolya, whom he succeeded. By 1541 Suleyman
the Magnificent had made Hungary a Turkish province, leaving John
as governor of Transylvania.

John IV (1604–56)
King of Portugal (1640–56)

Originally the Duke of Braganza, he became king when Portugal freed
itself from Spanish rule in 1640. Despite alliances with France,
Sweden, England and the Dutch, he was unable to secure Spanish
recognition of independent Portugal during his lifetime.

John II Casimir (1609–72)
King of Poland (1648–68)

The son of Sigismund III of Sweden and the brother of Ladislas IV,
whom he succeeded. A Swedish invasion forced him to flee to Silesia
and hostilities continued until the peace of Oliwa (1660). His efforts
to introduce constitutional reform (1660–1) were opposed by the
conservative opposition who raised a rebellion (1665–6). He
abdicated in 1668.

John III Sobieski (1624–96)
King of Poland (1674–96)

A native Pole of noble blood and a superb soldier. His entire reign
was spent campaigning against Tartar invaders and against the Turks.
In 1683, in alliance with Emperor Leopold I, he led the army that
defeated the Turks before Vienna, a victory that made him the hero
of Christian Europe.

Joseph II (1741–90)
Holy Roman Emperor (1765–90)

The son of Francis I, whom he succeeded — although his powers were limited until the death of his mother, Maria Theresa (1780). At the first partition of Poland (1772), he acquired Galicia, Lodomeria, and Zips; and in 1780 he appropriated a great part of Passau and Salzburg. In 1781 he published the Edict of Toleration for Protestants and Greeks. He also abolished serfdom, reorganized taxation, and stopped the feudal privileges of the nobles. In 1788 he engaged in an unsuccessful war with Turkey.

> So long as men obey the state, obey the laws and do not defame Your Majesty – what right have you to interfere in other things?
>
> *Joseph seeking to enlighten his mother Maria Theresa regarding religious toleration*

Juan Carlos I (1938–)
King of Spain (1975–)

The grandson of Spain's last ruling monarch, Alfonso XIII. He was educated in Switzerland and (from 1948) Spain. He married Princess Sophia of Greece (1962), who bore him three children. In 1969 Franco named him as his eventual successor, intending that he uphold the dictatorship. However when Juan Carlos became king, he presided over Spain's democratization, helped to defeat a military coup (1981), and assumed the role of a constitutional monarch.

Juliana, Louise Emma Marie Wilhelmina (1909–)
Queen of the Netherlands (1948–80)

She became a lawyer, and in 1937 married Prince Bernhard zur Lippe-Biesterfeld; they have four daughters. On the German invasion of Holland (1940), Juliana escaped to Britain and later lived in Canada. She returned to Holland in 1945, and became queen on the abdication of her mother, Wilhelmina. She in turn abdicated in favour of her eldest daughter, Beatrix.

k

Kenneth I or **Kenneth MacAlpin** (d.858)
King of the Scots (from 841) and of the Picts (from c.843)

He brought the territories of both peoples together in a united kingdom of Scotia (Scotland north of the Forth–Clyde line), and also moved the centre of the Church from Iona to Dunkeld.

Kristina (1626–89)
Queen of Sweden (1632–1654)

The daughter and successor of Gustavus II. When she came of age in 1644 she ended the costly war against the Denmark with the Peace of Westphalia in 1648. She patronized the arts, attracting to her court some of the best minds in Europe — among them Descartes. Refusing to marry, she chose her cousin, Charles X as her successor and in 1654 abdicated and became a Catholic. On the death of Charles X in 1660 she returned to Sweden, but failed to get herself reinstated.

L

Ladislas IV (1595–1648)
King of Poland (1632–48)

The son of Sigismund III Vasa of Sweden. His reign was peaceful, since Poland remained neutral during the Thirty Years War. At home, he crushed the Cossack rebellions (1637–8), establishing ten years of 'golden peace' in the Ukraine.

Leonidas (d.480 BC)
King of Sparta (c.491–480 BC)

A hero of the Persian Wars. He commanded a small force which, in an attempt to halt the Persian advance into central Greece, held the pass of Thermopylae for three days before being defeated by the Persians.

Leopold I (1790–1865)
King of the Belgians (1831–65)

The son of Francis, Duke of Saxe-Coburg. In 1816 he married Charlotte, daughter of the future George IV of England, and lived in England after her death (1817). He refused the crown of Greece (1830), but was then elected the first king of the Belgians. His second marriage, to Marie Louise of Orleans, daughter of Louis Philippe, ensured French support for his new kingdom against the Dutch, and his policies did much to keep Belgium free from European conflicts.

Leopold II (1835–1909)
King of the Belgians (1865–1909)

The son and successor of Leopold I. His chief interest was the expansion of Belgium abroad. In 1879 he founded a company to develop the Congo, and in 1885 became king of the Congo Free

State, which was annexed to Belgium in 1908. He was succeeded by
his nephew, Charles I.

Leopold III (1901–83)
King of the Belgians (1934–51)

The son and successor of Albert I. On his own authority he ordered
the surrender of the Belgian army to the Germans (1940), thereby
exposing the British Expeditionary Force, of whom some 250,000
had to be withdrawn, chiefly from the beaches of Dunkirk. He was
then imprisoned in Belgium until 1944, and afterwards in Austria.
On his return to Belgium (1945) he was forced to abdicate in favour
of his son Baudouin.

Leopold I (1640–1705)
Holy Roman Emperor (1658–1705), King of Hungary (from 1655) and Bohemia (from 1656)

The second son of Emperor Ferdinand III, whom he succeeded. His
two wars with the Turks (1661–4 and 1682–99) left him in control
of nearly all of Hungary. In 1686 he joined with William of Orange
(later William III of Great Britain) to combat French expansionism in
Europe. He had two sons who both succeeded him as emperor,
Joseph I and Charles VI.

Llywelyn Ap Iorweth, the Great (d.1240)
Prince of Gwynedd in north Wales (1194–1240)

He seized power from his uncle in 1194, successfully maintained his
independence against King John and Henry III, and extended his
kingdom over most of Wales.

Louis I, the Pious (778–840)
King of Aquitaine (781–814) and emperor of the Western or Carolingian Empire (814–40)

The sole surviving son of Charlemagne. He attempted to secure his
succession by dividing his lands between his sons, Lothair, Pepin,
Louis 'the German' and Charles the Bald (Charles I of France), with
Lothair to be the emperor. After his death the empire disintegrated
as his sons fought for supremacy.

Louis II, the Stammerer (846–79)
King of France (from 877), of Maine (from 856) and of Aquitaine (from 867)

The second son of Charles I the Bald. He was often in revolt against his father, whom he succeeded with great difficulty as king.

Louis III (c.863–82)
King of France (879–82)

The eldest son of Louis II, on whose death he was proclaimed joint king with his brother Carloman. He took Francia and Neustria as his territories. After his short reign he was succeeded by Carloman.

Louis IV, d'Outremer (d.954)
King of France (936–54)

The son of Charles III and grandson of Louis II. His early life was spent in England, but he was recalled on the death of King Raoul, by Hugh the Great (father of Hugh Capet) from whose political domination he later managed to escape. He was succeeded by his son, Lothair IV, and his grandson Louis V.

Louis V, le Fainéant (c.967–87)
King of France (986–7)

The son of Lothair IV. He died heirless and was thus the last Carolingian ruler of France. The throne passed to Hugh Capet, the first of the Capetian line.

Louis VI, the Fat (1081–1137)
King of France (1108–37)

The son of Philip I, whom he succeeded. He campaigned constantly against the unruly nobles of the Ile-de-France and eventually re-established his authority over his lands. He greatly increased the power and prestige of the monarchy.

Louis VII (c.1120–1180)
King of France (1137–80)

The second son of Louis VI, whom he succeeded. He had his marriage to Eleanor, heiress of Aquitaine, annulled in 1152, whereupon Eleanor married Henry Plantagenet, who became Henry II of England

in 1154. Louis succeeded in keeping Henry II at bay, by enlisting the
help of the pope and encouraging rebellion within Henry's family.

> We in France have nothing except bread and wine and joy
>
> *Contrasting France to the perceived wealth of Henry II's England,*
> *from Walter Map's* De Nugis Curiallum

Louis VIII, the Lion (1187–1226)
King of France (1223–6)

The son and successor of Philip II. During his father's reign, he
participated in attacks on the English (1214, 1216). His short reign
was marked chiefly by the renewed Albigensian Crusade (1226),
which led to the eventual absorption of all Languedoc into the royal
domain.

Louis IX (1214–70)
King of France (1226–70)

The son of Louis VIII, whom he succeeded. He repelled an invasion
from Henry III of England, and in 1248 led the Seventh Crusade.
After returning to France (1254), he carried out legal reforms. He
set out on a new Crusade in 1270, but died of plague in Tunis. He
was canonized in 1297.

> You are no king since you cannot bring your people to justice nor
> punish offenders.
>
> *William Longespee, according to Matthew Paris in* Chronicle majora

Louis X, the Quarrelsome (1289–1316)
King of Navarre (1305–16) and of France (1314–16)

The son of Philip IV. During his brief reign, which was marked by
unrest among his barons, he was guided in his policy by Charles of
Valois.

Louis XI (1423–83)
King of France (1461–83)

After two unsuccessful attempts to depose his father, Charles VII, he
succeeded to the throne on his father's death. With a mixture of
force and diplomatic cunning, he broke the power of the nobility,
and by 1483 he had succeeded in uniting most of France under one

crown (with the exception of Brittany), and laid the foundations for absolute monarchy in France.

Louis XII (1462–1515)
King of France (1498–1515)

The cousin of Charles VIII, whom he succeeded. He proved a popular ruler, concerned to provide justice and avoid oppressive taxation. His Italian ambitions brought him into conflict with Ferdinand II of Castile and the Holy League. Although the emperor Maximilian's designs on Brittany were unsuccessful, Louis's forces were driven from Italy (1512) and defeated by an Anglo-Imperial alliance at the battle of Guinegate (1513). To ensure peace, Louis married Mary Tudor, sister of Henry VIII (1514).

Louis XIII (1601–43)
King of France (1610–43)

He succeeded to the throne on the assassination of his father, Henry IV, but even after he came of age (1614) the Queen Regent, Marie de Medici, excluded him from power. In 1615 he married Anne of Austria, daughter of Philip III of Spain, and in 1617 took control of government, exiling his mother to Blois (1619–20). He became dependent upon Cardinal Richelieu, his chief minister from 1624. In his later years France was victorious against the Habsburgs in the Thirty Years War.

Louis XIV, the Great (1638–1715)
King of France (1643–1715)

The son and successor of Louis XIII. During his minority (1643–51) France was ruled by his mother, Anne of Austria, and her chief minister, Cardinal Mazarin. In 1660 Louis married the Infanta Maria Theresa, elder daughter of Philip IV of Spain, through whom he later claimed the Spanish crown for his second grandson (Philip V). Obsessed with the greatness of France, he pursued aggressive foreign and commercial policies, particularly against the Dutch. However his major political rivals were the Austrian Habsburgs. His attempt to create a Franco-Spanish Bourbon power-base led to the formation of the Grand Alliance of England, the United Provinces, and the Habsburg Empire, and resulted in the War of the Spanish Succession (1701–13). He was determined to preserve the unity of the French state and the independence of the French Church, which led to conflict with the Jansenists, the Huguenots, and the papacy. Although his old age saw military disaster and the financial ravages of prolonged warfare, Louis is considered a great monarch whose splendid court and absolute power earned him the nickname of 'le Roi Soleil' (the Sun King). He was succeeded by his great-grandson Louis XV.

> I am the State.
>
>   *1655 Before the Parlement de Paris, 13 Apr*

Louis XV (1710–74)
King of France (1715–74)

The great-grandson of Louis XIV, whom he succeeded. He married Maria Leczczynska, daughter of the deposed King Stanisław I of Poland. From 1726 he was guided by Cardinal de Fleury, but after Fleury's death in 1744, he vowed to rule without a chief minister, allowing government to drift into the hands of ministerial factions, while he indulged in secret and unofficial diplomatic activity. This system (*le secret du roi*) brought confusion to French foreign policy, leading to three continental wars and the loss of the French colonies in America and India (1763). His attempt to introduce reforms in 1771 came too late and the decline in royal authority continued. He was succeeded by his grandson, Louis XVI.

Louis XVI (1754–93)
King of France (1774–92)

The grandson of Louis XV, whom he succeeded. To strengthen the Franco-Austrian alliance, he married (1770) Marie Antoinette, daughter of Empress Maria Theresa. His reign saw the country decline into social and economic crisis, but he failed to support the ministers (eg Turgot and Necker) who tried to introduce reforms. He also allowed France to become involved in the costly War of American Independence (1778–83). In 1789 he agreed to summon the Estates General, but, encouraged by the Queen, he resisted the National Assembly's demands for reform, and in October was brought with his family from Versailles to Paris as a hostage to the Revolutionary movement. Louis reluctantly approved the new constitution (Sep 1791), but by August 1792 he and his family were imprisoned, and in September the monarchy was abolished. He was

tried before the National Convention for plotting with foreign
powers, and was guillotined in Paris.

> I would rather let people interpret my silence than my words.
>
> *1793 To Malesherbes*

Louis (Charles) XVII (1785–95)
Titular King of France (1793–5)

The second son of Louis XVI. On his father's execution (Jan 1793)
he remained in the Temple prison in Paris, where he died. The
secrecy surrounding his last months led to rumours of his escape and
produced several claimants to his title.

Louis XVIII or Louis Stanislas Xavier, Count of Provence (1755–1824)
King of France (1814–24)

The younger brother of Louis XVI. He fled from Paris in June 1791,
taking refuge in England, where he became the focus for the Royalist
cause. On Napoleon's downfall (1814) he re-entered Paris, and
promised a constitutional charter. Briefly ousted by Napoleon's return
from Elba, he was restored in 1815. His reign was marked by the
introduction of parliamentary government with a limited franchise.

> *L'exactitude est la politesse des rois.*
> Punctuality is the politeness of kings.
>
> *Attrib*

Louis IV, the Bavarian (c.1283–1347)
Holy Roman Emperor (from 1328) and King of Germany (from 1314)

The son of Louis, Duke of Upper Bavaria. His election as king was
opposed by a rival candidate, Frederick, Duke of Austria, whom he
eventually defeated in battle at Mühldorf (1322). Although Pope John
XXII refused to recognize him as emperor, he received the imperial
crown from the people of Rome (1328) and set up an anti-pope,
Nicholas V (1328–30). A rival emperor, Charles IV, was elected a
year before Louis met his death while hunting.

Louis, or **Lajos, the Great** (1326–82)
King of Hungary (from 1342) and of Poland (from 1370)

The son of Charles Robert, whom he succeeded. Up to 1356 his reign was mostly devoted to campaigns against Queen Johanna of Naples. His ultimate lack of success in Italy was offset by his conquest of Dalmatia, including the port of Dubrovnik. He became king of Poland on the death of his uncle, Casimir III.

Louis Philippe (1773–1850)
King of the French (1830–48)

Known as 'the Citizen King', he was the eldest son of Philippe Egalité, Duke of Orléans. At the Revolution he renounced his titles and joined the army. In 1793 he deserted to the Austrians, returning to France in 1814. Following the July Revolution and Charles X's abdication (1830) he was given the title of King of the French. However, political corruption and economic depression caused discontent, and when the Paris mob rose (1848), he abdicated and escaped to England.

Ludwig I (1786–1868)
King of Bavaria (1825–48)

His lavish expenditure, high taxes and reactionary policies caused risings in 1830, and again in 1848, when he abdicated in favour of his son, Maximilian II.

Ludwig II (1845–86)
King of Bavaria (1864–86)

The son of Maximilian II, whom he succeeded. In 1870 he sided with Prussia, though he took no part in the Franco-Prussian War. He was declared insane in 1886 and a few days later he was found drowned, with his physician, in the Starnberger Lake near his castle of Berg.

Ludwig III (1854–1921)
King of Bavaria (1913–18)

The son of the Prince Regent Luitpold. His five-year reign ended with his abdication. He was the last of the Wittelsbach family to occupy the throne.

m

Macbeth (c.1005–1057)
King of Scots (1040–57)

Probably a grandson of Kenneth II, and a nephew of Malcolm II. As provincial ruler of Moray, he overthrew and killed Duncan I in battle near Elgin (1040). Despite his malign Shakespearean image, he seems to have ruled wisely, avoiding expensive and debilitating raids on England. He became a benefactor of the Church and went on a pilgrimage to Rome (1050). He was defeated and killed at Lumphanan by Duncan's son, Malcolm III (Canmore), after an invasion from England aided by Earl Siward of Northumbria.

MacMurrogh, Dermot, correctly Diarmaid
Mac Murchadha (1110–71)
King of Leinster (1126–71)

Henry II of England allowed him to recruit allies among the Normans of Wales, the first of whom arrived in Ireland in 1169. Their leader Richard ('Strongbow') de Clare took Waterford, married Dermot's daughter Aoife, and with the Normans and Leinstermen captured the Norse city of Dublin. Strongbow succeeded Dermot in 1171 as ruler of Leinster, but was forced to resubmit to Henry II.

Magnus I, the Good (1024–47)
King of Norway (1035–47) and Denmark (1042–7)

The illegitimate son of King Olav II (St Olav). He came to the throne of Norway five years after his father's death at the battle of Stiklestad, and on the death of Hardicanute in 1042 he also inherited the Danish throne. In 1045 he agreed to share the throne of Norway with his uncle Harold III.

Magnus III, Barelegs (c.1074–1103)
King of Norway (1093–1103)

The son of King Olav III. He strengthened Norway's hold over her
North Sea territories, raiding the Orkneys and Shetland (1098–9),
and leading a naval expedition to Scotland and Ireland (1102–3). He
earned his nickname because he abandoned Norse trousers in favour
of the Scottish kilt.

Magnus V (1156–84)
King of Norway (1162–84)

The son of Earl Erling the Crooked. After his father's death in 1179
he was engaged in a long war against a rival claimant to the throne,
Sverrir Sigurdsson, and was forced to flee to Denmark. He died in
battle, attempting to regain his kingdom.

Magnus VI, the Law-Reformer (1238–80)
King of Norway (1263–80)

The son and successor of Haakon IV. He made peace with King
Alexander III of Scotland, to whom he surrendered the Western Isles
and the Isle of Man, and revised the laws of the land in a series of
legal codes based on Mercy, Truth, Fairness and Peace.

Magnus VII (1316–74)
King of Sweden (1319–64) and Norway (1319–55)

He succeeded his grandfather Haakon V as King of Norway and his
deposed uncle, Birger, as King of Sweden. In 1355 he handed over
Norway to his younger son, Haakon VI, and in the following year
was temporarily deposed in Sweden by his elder son, Erik (XII). After
Erik's death in 1359 he returned to power, but in 1364 was again
deposed — by the Swedish nobility. He was succeeded by his German
nephew, Albert of Mecklenburg.

Malcolm I (d.954)
King of Scotland (943–54)

The son of Donald II.

Malcolm II (c.954–1034)
King of Scotland (1016–34)

The son of Kenneth II.

Malcolm III or Malcolm Canmore (c.1031–93)
King of Scots (1058–93)

The son of Duncan I. He returned from exile (1054) and conquered S Scotland, but did not become king until he had defeated and killed Macbeth (who had killed his father), and disposed of Macbeth's stepson, Lulach. His second wife, the English princess Margaret (later St Margaret), was the sister of Edgar the Atheling, a claimant to the English throne. He died in battle at Alnwick, having invaded England five times during the period 1061–93.

Malcolm IV (c.1141–65)
King of Scots (1153–65)

The grandson and successor of David I. He was forced to restore the N English counties to Henry II in return for the earldom of Huntingdon (1157), then served on Henry's expedition to Toulouse (1159). He defeated Fergus, Lord of Galloway, in 1161 and Somerled, Lord of Argyll, in 1164. His nickname, 'the Maiden', refers to his reputation for chastity.

Manfred (1232–66)
King of Sicily (1258–66)

The illegitimate son of the emperor Frederick II. He was regent in Italy for his half-brother, Conrad IV, and his nephew Conradin of Swabia. In 1257 he defeated the pope's troops, and became master of Naples and Sicily. On the (false) rumour of Conradin's death (1258) he was crowned king. Pope Urban IV responded by giving Sicily to Charles of Anjou (brother of Louis IX of France), who defeated Manfred in battle at Benevento.

Manuel I or Emanuel (1469–1521)
King of Portugal (1495–1521)

Known as 'Emanuel the Great' or 'the Fortunate'. His reign marked a golden age for Portugal, spoiled only by his persecution of the Jews. He prepared the code of laws which bears his name; made his court a centre of chivalry, art, and science; and by sponsoring the voyages of Vasco da Gama, Cabral, and others, helped to establish Portugal as the first naval power of Europe and a world centre of commerce.

Manuel II (1889–1932)
King of Portugal (1908–10)

He became king on the assassination of his father King Carlos I and the Crown Prince Luis, but was forced to abdicate at the revolution of 3 October 1910.

Margaret (1353–1412)
Queen of Denmark (from 1375), Norway (from 1380) and Sweden (from 1389)

She became Queen of Denmark on the death of her father, Waldemar IV, and ruled Norway from the death of her husband, Haakon VI. In 1388 she supported a rising of Swedish nobles against their king, Albert of Mecklenburg, and became Queen of Sweden. Her young cousin, Erik of Pomerania, was crowned king of the three kingdoms at Kalmar in 1397, but Margaret remained the real ruler of Scandinavia until her death.

Margaret, the 'Maid of Norway' (1283–90)
Infant queen of Scotland (1286–90)

The only child of Margaret (daughter of Alexander III of Scotland) and Erik II of Norway. She succeeded Alexander III on his death in 1286, and in 1289 was betrothed to the infant Prince Edward (the future Edward II of England). She died at sea the following year on her way from Norway to the Orkneys.

Margaret of Anjou (1429–82)
Queen-consort of Henry VI of England

The daughter of René of Anjou. Because of Henry's madness, she became involved in political life, and was a leading Lancastrian during the Wars of the Roses. Defeated at Tewkesbury (1471), she was imprisoned in the Tower for four years, until ransomed by Louis XI.

Margaret of Austria (1480–1530)
Regent of the Netherlands

The daughter of Emperor Maximilian I. She married the Infante Juan of Spain (1497), and then Philibert II, Duke of Savoy (1501). In 1507 her father appointed her regent of the Netherlands and guardian of her nephew, the future emperor Charles V.

Margaret Tudor (1489–1541)
Queen-consort of James IV of Scotland

The eldest daughter of Henry VII. She married James IV (1503) and
was the mother of James V, for whom she acted as regent. She was
involved in political intrigues between the pro-French and pro-English
factions in Scotland, but was discredited (1534) when James
discovered that she had betrayed state secrets to her brother, Henry
VIII of England.

Margrethe II (1940–)
Queen of Denmark (1972–)

The daughter of Frederick IX. She qualified as an archaeologist, then
in 1967 married a French diplomat, Count Henri de Laborde de
Monpezat (now Prince Henrik of Denmark). Their children are the
heir apparent Prince Frederik André Henrik Christian (1968–) and
Prince Joachim Holger Waldemar Christian (1969–).

Maria Theresa (1717–80)
Archduchess of Austria, Queen of Hungary and Bohemia
(1740–80) and Holy Roman Empress

The daughter of Emperor Charles VI. In 1736 she married Francis,
Duke of Lorraine (who became Holy Roman Emperor in 1745), and
in 1740 succeeded to the hereditary Habsburg lands — triggering the
War of the Austrian Succession (1741–8), in which she lost Silesia to
Frederick II of Prussia. The Seven Years War (1756–63) further
confirmed her loss of Silesia. During her later years she strove to
maintain international peace, and reluctantly accepted the partition
of Poland. She was succeeded by her eldest son, Joseph II.

Marie Antoinette (Josèphe Jeanne) (1755–93)
Queen of France

The daughter of Emperor Francis I and Maria Theresa, and wife (from
1770) of the Dauphin of France (later Louis XVI). She was criticized
for her extravagance and opposition to reform. From the outbreak of
the French Revolution, she resisted the advice of constitutional
monarchists (eg Comte de Mirabeau). In June 1791 she and Louis
tried to escape to her native Austria, but were captured at Varennes,

imprisoned in Paris, and guillotined.

> *Qu'ils mangent de la brioche.*
> Let them eat cake.
>
>> *Her response to the complaints of her people about the lack of bread*

Marie de Medici (1573–1642)
Queen-consort of Henry IV of France

The daughter of Francesco de Medici, Grand Duke of Tuscany. She married Henry in 1600, and gave birth to the future Louis XIII in 1601. After Henry's assassination (1610) she acted as regent, but when Louis assumed royal power (1617) he imprisoned her at Blois. She continued to plot against Louis and was banished to Compiègne, but escaped to Brussels (1631), and spent her last years in poverty.

Mary I (1516–58)
Queen of England and Ireland (1553–8)

The daughter of Henry VIII by his first wife, Catherine of Aragon. A devout Catholic, she lived in retirement during the reign of her half-brother Edward VI. Despite Northumberland's attempts to prevent her succession on Edward's death, with the support of the country she entered London and ousted Lady Jane Grey. She then repealed anti-Catholic laws and revived Catholic practices, intending to restore the authority of the pope and to marry the Catholic Philip II of Spain. She responded to the Wyatt rebellion by executing Lady Jane Grey and imprisoning her own half-sister Elizabeth. Mary's unpopular marriage to Philip (1554) was followed by the persecution of some 300 Protestants, which earned her the name 'Bloody Mary'. Broken by childlessness, sickness, grief at her husband's departure from England, and the loss of Calais to the French, she died in London.

> When I am dead and opened, you shall find 'Calais' lying in my heart.
>
>> *1808* Holinshed's Chronicles *vol 4*

Mary II (1662–94)
Queen of Great Britain and Ireland (1689–94)

The daughter of James II and Anne Hyde. She married (1677) her cousin, William, Stadtholder of the United Netherlands. On the invitation of seven Whig peers, William landed in England with an Anglo-Dutch army (1688) and James II fled to France. Mary shared the throne with her husband (who became King William III), but in fact ruled only when he was abroad or campaigning in Ireland.

Mary of Modena, née d'Este (1658–1718)
Queen-consort of James II of Great Britain and Ireland

The daughter of Alfonso IV, Duke of Modena. She married James in 1673 and in 1688 gave birth to their only surviving child, James Francis Edward Stewart (the future 'Old Pretender'). When William of Orange (the future William III) landed in England later that year, she escaped to France with her infant son, to be joined there later by her deposed husband.

Mary (of Teck), known as Princess May (1867–1953)
Queen-consort of George V of Great Britain

The daughter of Francis, Duke of Teck, and Princess Mary Adelaide of Cambridge. She married Prince George, Duke of York, in 1893, and they had five sons and one daughter. After his accession (as George V) in 1910, she helped to mould her husband into a 'people's king' and after the abdication of her eldest son, Edward VIII, she did much to restore the dignity of the monarchy throughout the reign of her second son, George VI.

Mary, Queen of Scots (1542–87)
Queen of Scotland (virtually from birth to her forced abdication in 1567) and Queen-consort of Francis II of France (1559–60)

The daughter of James V of Scotland and Mary of Guise. After the Scots' defeat at Pinkie (1547), she was sent to France where she married the Dauphin (later Francis II) in 1558. She returned to Scotland a widow in 1561. Her designs on the English throne led her to marry her cousin, Henry Stuart, Lord Darnley, a grandson of Margaret Tudor (1565), but she soon grew to hate him. The vicious murder of Rizzio, her Italian secretary, by Darnley and a group of Protestant nobles (1566) deepened her disgust, and the birth of the future James VI failed to bring reconciliation. When Darnley was killed, the chief suspect, the Earl of Bothwell, was acquitted and afterwards married Mary. The Protestant nobles then rose against her. They imprisoned Mary at Lochleven and forced her to abdicate.

Mary escaped, raised an army, but was defeated again at Langside
(1568). She placed herself under the protection of Queen Elizabeth,
but was instead made a prisoner for life. Her presence in England
gave rise to many plots to depose Elizabeth and restore Catholicism.
Finally, after the Babington conspiracy (1586) she was brought to
trial for treason, and executed in Fotheringay Castle,
Northamptonshire.

Matthias I Corvinus (c.1443–1490)
King of Hungary (1458–90)

He was elected in 1458, but six years' struggle against Turks,
Bohemians and the emperor Frederick III followed, before he could
be crowned. He drove back the Turks, made himself master of Bosnia
(1462) and of Moldavia and Wallachia (1467), and in 1478 agreed a
peace treaty with Ladislaus of Bohemia. Out of this war grew another
with Frederick III, in which Matthias captured Vienna (1485) and a
large part of Austria proper.

Maximilian I (1459–1519)
Holy Roman Emperor (1493–1519)

The son and successor of Emperor Frederick III. His foreign policy
was based on marriage alliances and had far-reaching results for
Habsburg power. His marriage to Mary of Burgundy brought his
family the Burgundian inheritance, including the Netherlands, while
the marriage of his son Philip with the Infanta Joanna meant that the
Spanish Crown passed to his grandson, Charles V (1516). Another
double marriage treaty led to the union of Austria–Bohemia–Hungary
(1526). He was involved in conflicts with the Flemish, the Swiss and
German princes and especially with the Valois kings of France. He
was succeeded by his grandson Charles V.

Maximilian II (1527–76)
King of Bohemia (from 1548) and Holy Roman Emperor
(from 1564)

The son of Emperor Ferdinand I and Anna of Bohemia and Hungary.
He embarrassed his family by his Protestant leanings and was obliged
in 1562 to swear to live and die within the Catholic Church. As
emperor he secured considerable religious freedom for Austrian
Lutherans.

Michael (1921–)
King of Romania (1927–30, 1940–7)

The son of Carol II. He came to the throne on the death of his grandfather Ferdinand I, since his father had renounced his own claims in 1925. Although Carol deposed him in 1930, Michael was restored to the throne when the Germans gained control of Romania (1940). In 1944 he led a coup to overthrow the dictatorship of Antonescu, and declared war on Germany, but was forced to accept a communist-dominated government (1945) and later to abdicate (1947).

Michael Romanov (1596–1676)
Tsar of Russia (1613–45)

The great-nephew of Ivan the Terrible. He was the founder of the Romanov dynasty that ruled Russia until the revolution of 1917, elected during the 'Time of Troubles' that had plagued Russia since the death of Boris Godunov in 1605. He concluded peace with Sweden (1617) and Poland (1618).

Miguel, Maria Evaristo de Branganza (1802–66)
King of Portugal (1828–34)

The third son of King John VI. He was banished (1824) for plotting to overthrow the constitutional government. On John's death in 1826 the crown passed to Miguel's elder brother, Pedro I, who abdicated in favour of his daughter, Maria de Gloria, making Miguel regent. Miguel had himself proclaimed king in 1828, but was defeated in the war that followed and Maria was restored in 1834.

Murat, Joachim (1767–1815)
King of Naples (1808–15)

A distinguished cavalry officer in the French army, in 1799 he helped Napoleon become First Consul, and in 1800 married Napoleon's sister, Caroline. He was proclaimed king of the Two Sicilies (1808), and took possession of Naples. In an attempt to keep his throne after Napoleon's defeat at Leipzig (1813), he made a treaty with Austria — which he promptly broke on Napoleon's return from Elba. Twice defeated, he lost Naples and was captured and executed in Pizzo, Calabria.

n

Napoleon I or Napoléon Bonaparte (1769–1821)
French Emperor (1804–15)

During the Revolutionary Wars he was appointed commander of the French army in Italy (1796) and in the same year married Josephine, widow of the Vicomte de Beauharnais. Hoping to break British trade by conquering Egypt, he took Cairo, but after Nelson destroyed the French fleet at the battle of Aboukir Bay, Napoleon returned to France, where he seized power (9 Nov 1799) as First Consul. The Concordat with Rome and the Peace of Amiens confirmed his position, and in 1804 he took the title of Emperor. War with England was renewed, and spread to Russia, Austria and Prussia. Defeated at Trafalgar (1805), he gained victories at Ulm, Austerlitz, Jena, Auerstadt (1806) and Friedland (1807). In Portugal and Spain (the Peninsular War, 1808–14), his armies were finally defeated by the British forces under the Duke of Wellington. His invasion of Russia ended in the disastrous retreat from Moscow, in which his army was broken by the Russian winter. In 1813 he was routed at Leipzig and forced to abdicate. Sent to rule Elba in 1814, he returned to France in 1815 and regained power for a period known as 'the Hundred Days'. Defeated at Waterloo, he was banished to St Helena where he died. His son by his second wife, Marie Louise, daughter of the Emperor of Austria, was briefly proclaimed Napoleon II in 1815.

> An army marches on its stomach.
>
> *Attrib*

Napoleon III (1808–73)
Emperor of the French (1852–70)

Born Charles Louis Napoleon Bonaparte, he was the third son of Louis Bonaparte, King of Holland, and nephew of Napoleon I. After the death of Napoleon II (1832) he became head of the Napoleonic dynasty. He made two attempts on the French throne (1836, 1840) for which he was imprisoned, but after the 1848 Revolution was elected president of the Second Republic. With the help of the military, he overthrew the constitution, and took the title of Emperor. In 1870 he unwisely declared war on Prussia, was defeated and passed the rest of his life in exile.

Nicholas I (1796–1855)
Emperor of Russia (1825–55)

The third son of Paul I. An absolute despot, he warred with Persia and Turkey, suppressed a rising in Poland, and tried to make all the inhabitants of his empire adopt the Russian language and culture. He helped to crush the 1848 Hungarian revolt and tightened the alliance with Prussia. However, his attempts to overrun Turkey roused the opposition of Britain and France and triggered the Crimean War. He was succeeded by his son, Alexander II.

> He is stern and severe — with fixed principles of duty which nothing on earth will make him change.
>
> *Queen Victoria*

Nicholas II (1868–1918)
Emperor of Russia (1894–1917)

The son and successor of Alexander III. His reign was marked by an alliance with France (1894), an entente with Britain, a disastrous war with Japan (1904–5), the Revolution of 1905 (precipitated by inadequate industrialization and social change) and the establishment of the national assembly or Duma (1906). His failure to concede any real power to the Duma, however, and also his incompetence as commander of the Russian armies against the Central Powers (Germany and Austria–Hungary) in 1915, helped bring about the 1917 Russian Revolution. Forced to abdicate, he was shot with his family by the Red Guards at Ekaterinburg in 1918.

> I shall maintain the principle of autocracy just as firmly and unflinchingly as it was upheld by my own, ever to be remembered dead father.
>
> *1896 Declaration, 17 Jan*

O

Odoacer or Odovacer (c.433–93 AD)
King of Italy (AD 476–93)

A Germanic warrior who destroyed the W Roman Empire, and became the first barbarian king of Italy. He was challenged and overthrown by the Ostrogothic king Theodoric (489–93), at the request of the E Roman emperor, Zeno.

Offa (d.796)
King of Mercia (757–96)

He called himself 'King of the English', and asserted his authority over all the kingdoms south of the Humber, treating their rulers as provincial governors and earning Charlemagne's respect. He constructed Offa's Dyke (which marks the western boundary of his kingdom with Wales) between 784 and 786, and introduced a new currency based on the silver penny. The Mercian supremacy collapsed soon after his death.

Olav I (c.965–1000)
King of Norway (995–1000)

The great-grandson of Harold I. In 994 he took part in Sweyn Forkbeard's expedition against England. While in England he was converted to Christianity and in the following year he returned to Norway, where he seized the throne and attempted to convert Norway to Christianity by force. He was overthrown by a combined Danish and Swedish force at the battle of Svold.

Olav II (St Olav) (c.995–1030)
King of Norway (1014–28)

The half-brother of Harold III. He was converted to Christianity in

Normandy in 1013, and returned to Norway in 1014, where he seized the throne and worked to complete the conversion of Norway begun by Olav I. A rebellion in 1028 forced him into exile. Two years later, he attempted to regain his crown, but was defeated and killed at the battle of Stiklestad. He is the patron saint of Norway.

Olav III, the Peaceful (d.1093)
King of Norway (1067–93)

The son of Harold III. He was at the battle of Stamford Bridge in Yorkshire in 1066 when his father was defeated and killed by Harold II of England, but was allowed to return to Norway. His long reign was marked by unbroken peace and prosperity. He was succeeded by his illegitimate son, Magnus III.

Olav V (1903–91)
King of Norway (1957–91)

The only child of Haakon VII and Maud, daughter of Edward VII. Appointed head of the Norwegian armed forces in 1944, he escaped with his father to England on the Nazi occupation, but returned in 1945. In 1929 he married Princess Martha (1901–54) of Sweden, and had two daughters and a son, Harald (1937–   ), who succeeded to the Norwegian throne as Harald V.

Olympias (d.316 BC)
Macedonian queen

The wife of Philip II of Macedon, and mother of Alexander the Great. When Philip divorced her, she left Macedon but returned after Alexander's death in 323 BC to install his son, Alexander IV, as king. She was put to death by Cassander.

Oskar I (1799–1859)
King of Sweden and Norway (1844–59)

The only son and successor of Charles XIV. He encouraged social and economic reforms, and followed a policy of Scandinavian unity and Swedish neutrality. He was succeeded by his eldest son, Charles XV.

Oskar II (1829–1907)
King of Sweden (1872–1907) and Norway (1872–1905)

He was the younger son of Oskar I and brother of Charles XV, whom he succeeded. He served as mediator in international disputes, but found it impossible to keep the union of Norway and Sweden intact, and in 1905 surrendered the crown of Norway to Prince Carl of Denmark (Haakon VII). He was succeeded as king of Sweden by his son, Gustavus V.

St Oswald (c.605–42)
King of Northumbria (633–41)

The son of Ethelfrith of Bernicia. He was converted at Iona, then established Christianity in Northumbria with the help of the Celtic monk St Aidan. He fell in battle with the pagan king Penda.

Otto I, the Great (912–73)
King of the Germans (from 936) and Holy Roman Emperor (from 962)

The son of Henry I, the Fowler, whom he succeeded as King of Germany. He subdued many turbulent tribes, maintained almost supreme power in Italy, and encouraged Christian missions to Scandinavian and Slavonic lands.

Otto IV (c.1174–1218)
Holy Roman Emperor (1209-1214)

The son of Henry the Lion. He was elected king in 1198, but was in conflict with a rival claimant, Philip of Swabia, for ten years. After Philip's murder in 1208 he was crowned emperor, but his subsequent invasion of Sicily lost him the support of Pope Innocent III who raised up Philip's nephew, Frederick II, as a rival. He was defeated by Philip II of France at the battle of Bouvines (1214).

p

Parr, Catherine (1512–48)
English queen, the sixth wife of Henry VIII

The daughter of Sir Thomas Parr of Kendal. She married first Edward
Borough, then Lord Latimer, before she became Queen of England
(1643). A learned and tactful woman, she persuaded Henry to restore
the succession to his daughters. Shortly after Henry's death (1547)
she married a former suitor, Lord Thomas Seymour of Sudeley, and
died in childbirth the following year.

Paul I (1901–64)
King of Greece (1947–64)

When Greece became a republic (1924) he went into exile, returning
as Crown Prince in 1935. He served with the Greek general staff in
the Albanian campaign in World War II, and was a member of the
Greek government in exile in London (1941–6). His reign was
marked by the Greek Civil War (1946–9) and its difficult aftermath.
He was succeeded by his son, Constantine II.

Paul (1754–1801)
Emperor of Russia (1796–1801)

The son of Peter III and Catherine the Great. He first backed the
coalition against France, but then quarrelled with England and entered
into an alliance with Napoleon. He was murdered by his own officers,
and was succeeded by his son, Alexander I.

Pedro, the Cruel (1334–69)
King of Castile and Leon (1349–69)

The son and successor of Alfonso XI. He put down a revolt in favour
of his illegitimate brother Henry of Trestamara in 1354, and with the
help of Edward the Black Prince defeated his rival at Najera in 1367.

However, following Edward's departure from Spain, Pedro was routed and killed by Henry at Montiel.

Penda (c.575–655)
King of Mercia (c.632–55)

He mastered the English Midlands, and frequently warred with the kings of Northumbria. His forces defeated and killed Edwin at Hatfield in Yorkshire (633), and also Edwin's successor, Oswald, when he invaded Penda's territories (642). Penda was slain in battle near Leeds while campaigning against Oswald's successor, Oswiu.

Pepin (777–810)
King of Italy (781–810)

The second son of Charlemagne. He fought against the Avars, Slavs, Saxons and Saracens.

Pepin III, the Short (c.715–68)
King of the Franks (751–68)

The father of Charlemagne. He became the first Carolingian king of the Franks after the deposition of Childeric, the last of the Merovingians. He led an army into Italy (754), and defeated the Lombards. The rest of his life was spent in wars against the Saxons and Saracens.

Perseus (c.213–c.165 BC)
King of Macedon (179–168 BC)

The son of Philip V, whom he succeeded. In the Third Macedonian War (171–168 BC), he was defeated at the battle of Pydna (168 BC) and taken to Italy, where he died in captivity. The monarchy of Macedon was then abolished.

Peter I, the Great (1672–1725)
Tsar of Russia (1682–1721) and Emperor of Russia (1721–5)

The son of Tsar Alexey and his second wife Natalia Naryshkin. On the death of Ivan V(1696), his mentally retarded half-brother with whom he had been joint tsar under the regency of his half-sister Sophia, he embarked on a series of sweeping reforms, many of them based on W European models. All classes of society suffered as a result — his own son Alexey died under torture (1718), suspected of plotting against his father. Peter fought major wars with the Ottoman Empire, Persia, and in particular Sweden, which Russia defeated in the Great Northern War. This victory established Russia as a major European power, and gained access to the Baltic coast, where Peter founded St Petersburg. He was succeeded by his wife Catherine I.

> We must not lose our heads in misfortune.
>> *Letter to Boris Sheremetev on hearing of Charles XII's victory at the battle of Narva*

Peter II (1715–30)
Tsar of Russia (1727–30)

The grandson of Peter the Great, he succeeded to the throne on the death of his step-grandmother, Catherine I. He died of smallpox on the day set for his wedding and was succeeded by the empress Anna Ivanova.

Peter III (1728–62)
Tsar of Russia (1762)

The grandson of Peter the Great. In 1745 he married Sophia-Augusta von Anhalt-Zerbst (the future Catherine II the Great). He succeeded his aunt, the empress Elizabeth Petrovna, in January 1762, and immediately withdrew Russia from the Seven Years War and restored East Prussia to Frederick II. This enraged the army and aristocracy, and in June Peter was deposed and murdered by a group of nobles led by his wife's lover, Count Orlov. A few days later Catherine was proclaimed empress.

Peter I (1844–1921)
King of Serbia (1903–21)

In World War I he accompanied his army into exile in Greece in 1916. He returned to Belgrade in 1918 and was proclaimed titular king of the Serbs, Croats and Slovenes until his death, although his second son, Alexander (later Alexander I), was regent.

Peter II (1923–70)
King of Yugoslavia (1934–45)

The son of Alexander I. After his father was assassinated in 1934, his uncle, Prince Paul Karadjordjevic, was regent until 1941 when he was ousted by pro-Allied army officers, who declared King Peter of age. He set up a government in exile in London, but lost his throne when Yugoslavia became a republic in 1945.

Philip I (1052–1108)
King of France (1067–1108)

The son of Henry I. His reign marked a low point in the prestige of the monarchy, mainly because he eloped with Bertrada, wife of Fulk of Anjou, causing a scandal which led to his excommunication. He was succeeded by his son, Louis VI.

Philip II (1165–1223)
King of France (1180–1223)

The son of Louis VII, whom he succeeded. His reign was important to the development of the medieval kingdom of France, for although he embarked on the Third Crusade in 1190, he returned the following year to concentrate on attacking the continental lands belonging to King John of England. By the time he died most of France was under his control.

Philip III, the Bold (1245–85)
King of France (1270–85)

He was with his father, Louis IX, at his death in Tunis (1270), and fought several unlucky campaigns in Spain, the last of which, the attack on Aragon, resulted in his death.

Philip IV, the Fair (1268–1314)
King of France (1285–1314)

The son and successor of Philip III. Through his marriage with Joanna of Navarre, he gained control over Navarre, Champagne and Brie, but his efforts to overrun Flanders ended in defeat at Courtrai (1302). His conflict with the papacy led him to imprison Pope Boniface VIII and in 1305 he secured the election of Pope Clement V, who came to reside at Avignon. He forced the pope to dissolve the order of the

Knights Templar, whose property he seized (1314). He was succeeded by his son, Louis X.

Philip V, the Tall (1293–1322)
King of France (1316–22)

The second son of Philip IV and brother of Louis X, whom he succeeded. He ended the war with Flanders (1320), and tried to unify the coinage. He was succeeded by his brother, Charles IV.

Philip VI (1293–1350)
King of France (1328–50)

The nephew of Philip IV. He became the first Valois king of France on the death of Charles IV, but his succession was contested by Edward III of England, son of Philip IV's daughter, who declared that females, though excluded by the Salic law, could pass their rights to their children. Thus began the Hundred Years War with England (1337). In 1346 Edward III defeated Philip at Crécy, just as the Black Death was about to spread through France.

Philip II (382–336 BC)
King of Macedonia (359–336 BC)

He created the unified state of Macedonia (359–353 BC), established its military and economic power, and defeated the Greeks at Chaeronea (338 BC). The planned Macedonian conquest of Persia, cut short by his assassination in 336 BC, was eventually carried out by his son, Alexander the Great.

Philip V (238–179 BC)
King of Macedonia (221–179 BC)

The adopted heir of Antigonus Doson. His alliance with Hannibal during the Second Punic War led to the First Macedonian War (214–205 BC) with Rome. The Second Macedonian War (200–196 BC) resulted in Philip's defeat at Cynoscephalae in 197 BC, and he had to give up all control of Greece. He was succeeded by his son Perseus.

Philip I, the Handsome (1478–1506)
King of Castile (1506)

The son of Emperor Maximilian I and Mary of Burgundy. In 1496 he married the Infanta of Spain, Joanna, daughter of Ferdinand and

Isabella. When Joanna became queen of Castile on Isabella's death (1504) Ferdinand promptly declared himself her regent. In 1506 Philip went to claim the throne, but died in the same year. Joanna became insane and was imprisoned by her father.

Philip II (1527–98)
King of Spain (1556–98) and Portugal (as Philip I, 1580–98)

The only son of Emperor Charles V and Isabella of Portugal. After the death of his first wife, Maria of Portugal, he married Mary I (1554) and became joint sovereign of England. By the time of Mary's death (1558), he had inherited the Habsburg possessions in Italy, the Netherlands, Spain, and the New World. A champion of the Counter-Reformation, he tried to destroy infidels and heretics, and to crush Protestantism, first in the Low Countries (from 1568), then in England and France. His reign was marked by the destruction of the Armada (1588), the continuing revolt of the Netherlands, economic problems, and internal unrest, but there were political achievements in the reduction of Ottoman seapower after the battle of Lepanto (1571) and the conquest of Portugal (1580). He was succeeded by his son, Philip III.

> Your Majesty spends so long considering your undertakings that when the moment to perform them comes the occasion has passed and the money all been spent.
>
> *Pius V*

Philip III (1578–1621)
King of Spain and, as Philip II, of Portugal (1598–1621)

The son of Philip II, whom he succeeded. He left government to corrupt ministers and devoted himself to the interests of the church. Agriculture and industry declined, and foreign wars drained the treasury. In 1606 the Moriscos (Muslim converts to Christianity) were expelled from Spain. He was succeeded by his son, Philip IV.

Philip IV (1605–65)
King of Spain (1621–65) and of Portugal (1621–40)

The son of Philip III, whom he succeeded. His reign continued the rapid decline of Spain as a dominant European power. Portugal regained its independence (1640); Holland was lost by the Treaty of

Westphalia (1648); and the Treaty of the Pyrenees cost Spain its frontier fortresses in Flanders (1659). He was succeeded by his son, Charles II, the last of the Habsburgs.

Philip V (1683–1746)
King of Spain (1700–46)

The grandson of Louis XIV of France, and great-grandson of Philip IV of Spain. After a long struggle with the Habsburg rival for the Spanish succession, he gained the throne at the Peace of Utrecht (1713), but lost the Spanish Netherlands and Italian territories. Influenced by his second wife, Elizabeth Farnese of Parma, he attempted to regain his Italian lands, but was out-matched by an alliance between Austria, Great Britain, France, and the United Provinces.

Podiebrad, George of (1420–71)
King of Bohemia (1458–71)

A member of the Czech nobility and leader of the Ultraquists (moderate Protestant followers of Jan Huss). He seized Prague (1448), and had himself made regent (1453–7) for the young Ladislaus Posthumus, on whose death he became king. In 1469 the Catholic barons crowned Matthias Corvinus of Hungary as a rival king, and in 1478 a peace treaty was agreed, whereby Matthias Corvinus and Podiebrad's successor, Ladislaus, would both retain the title.

Pyrrhus (c.318–272 BC)
King of Epirus (modern Albania) (307–303 BC, 297–272 BC)

He came into conflict with Rome when he supported Tarentum (a Greek colony in southern Italy) against the Romans. Though he won two battles against Rome at Tarentum and Asculum (280–279 BC), his losses were so heavy that they gave rise to the phrase 'Pyrrhic victory'.

R

Richard I, the Lionheart (1157–99)
King of England (1189–99)

The third son of Henry II and Eleanor of Aquitaine. For most of his reign he was crusading and defending the Angevin lands against Philip II of France, spending only five months in England. He took Messina (1190), Cyprus, and Acre (1191) during the Third Crusade, and advanced to within sight of Jerusalem, but on his return was arrested at Vienna (1192), and remained a prisoner of the German emperor Henry VI until he agreed to be ransomed (1194).

> . . . the finest knight / On earth, and the most skilled to fight.
> *Norman author of verse* Estoire de la Guerre Sainte

Richard II (1367–1400)
King of England (1377–99)

The son of Edward the Black Prince and grandson of Edward III, whom he succeeded. He showed great bravery in confronting the rebels in London during the Peasants' Revolt (1381). He quarrelled with Parliament, notably his uncle, John of Gaunt, and his main supporters were found guilty of treason in the 'Merciless Parliament' of 1388. In 1397–8 he took his revenge by having the Earl of Arundel executed, the Duke of Gloucester murdered, and several lords banished, including Gaunt's son, Henry Bolingbroke (later Henry IV). Throughout Richard's reign the magnates had tried to limit his power, and since they had failed by constitutional means, Bolingbroke invaded England unopposed and took his throne (Sep 1399).

Richard III (1452–85)
King of England (1483–5)

The youngest son of Richard, Duke of York. He was created Duke of Gloucester by his brother, Edward IV, in 1461, accompanied him into exile (1470), and played a key role in his restoration (1471). He was given viceregal powers in N England, and in 1482 recaptured Berwick-upon-Tweed from the Scots. When Edward died (1483) and was succeeded by his under-age son, Edward V, Richard acted first as protector, but before long had himself crowned king. Young Edward and his brother were probably murdered in the Tower on Richard's orders. He died in battle at Bosworth Field, fighting his rival, Henry Tudor (later Henry VII).

> The Cat, the Rat and Lovell our dog
> Rulen all England under an Hog.
>
> *1483 famous rhyme nailed to the door of St Paul's Cathedral,
> which alludes to the trio of advisors to Richard (namely Francis,
> Viscount Lovell, Sir Richard Ratcliffe and William Catesby)*

Robert I of Scotland see Bruce, Robert.

Robert II (1316–90)
King of Scots (1371–90)

The son of Walter. He acted as regent during the exile and captivity of David II. On David's death, he became king in right of his descent from his maternal grandfather, Robert Bruce, and founded the Stuart royal dynasty.

Robert III (c.1340–1406)
King of Scotland (1390–1406)

The son and successor of Robert II. Because he was an invalid, his son, David, Duke of Rothesay was appointed guardian of the kingdom in 1398. After Rothesay's murder in 1402, the king's brother, the Duke of Albany, came to power and Robert sent his younger son (the future James I) to France for safety. He died shortly after news arrived of James's capture by the English.

Robert of Anjou, the Wise (1278–1343)
King of Naples (1309–43)

The grandson of Charles of Anjou, and son of Charles II, whom he succeeded. A leader of the Guelf papal party, he nonetheless broke with Pope John XXII in 1330.

Roderic (d.711)
Visigothic king of Spain (710-11)

The last Visigothic king of Spain. He was elected on the death of Witiza, and died in battle against the invading Moors, who went on to conquer most of Spain.

Roger II (1095–1154)
King of Sicily (1130–54)

The son of Roger I. He united Sicily and S Italy in a strong Norman kingdom, adding to his dominions: Capua (1136), Naples and the Abruzzi (1140), Tripoli, Tunis and Algeria (1147). His court at Palermo was one of the most magnificent in Europe.

Romulus
Legendary first king of Rome

In Roman legend, the son of Mars and Rhea Silvia. He and his twin brother Remus were thrown in the Tiber, and when washed ashore, were suckled by a she-wolf. In 753 BC he founded his city, and in 716 BC was said to have been carried up to heaven in a chariot of fire.

Rudolf I (1218–91)
German King (1273–91)

The founder of the Habsburg dynasty. He increased his territories by inheritance and marriage until he was the most powerful prince in Swabia.

Rudolf II (d.937)
King of Burgundy (912–37)

The son of Rudolf I, whom he succeeded, and father of the empress St Adelaide. He became king of Italy in 922, but resigned the throne in 926 in return for Provence.

Rudolf III (d.1032)
Last king of Burgundy (993–1032)

The grandson of Rudolf II.

S

Sebastian (1554–78)
King of Portugal (1557–78)

The grandson of John III, whom he succeeded. He launched a futile
and costly war against the Moors of North Africa, and fell in the
battle of Alcazar-Qivir in Algeria. His death without an heir opened
the way for the union of Portugal with Spain under his uncle Philip
II of Spain.

Servius Tullius (578–535 BC)
Semi-legendary king of Rome

He is said to have divided all freeholders into tribes, classes and
centuries, making property, not birth, the standard of citizenship.

Seymour, Jane (c.1509–37)
English queen, the third wife of Henry VIII

The sister of Protector Somerset. A lady-in-waiting to Henry's first
two wives (Catherine of Aragon and Anne Boleyn), she married him
11 days after Anne's execution. She died soon after the birth of her
son, the future Edward VI.

Sigismund (1368–1437)
Holy Roman Emperor (from 1410), King of Hungary (from
1387), Germany (from 1411) and Bohemia (from 1419)

The son of Emperor Charles IV. In 1396 he was defeated by the
Ottoman Turks at Nicopolis, but later conquered Bosnia, Herzegovina
and Serbia. He persuaded the pope to call the Council of Constance
to end the Hussite schism (1414), but failed to provide the 'safe
conduct' he had granted John Huss, and allowed him to be burned.
This led to the refusal by the Hussites to recognize his succession in
Bohemia, and ultimately to the Hussite wars (1420–33)

Sigismund I, the Old (1467–1548)
King of Poland (1506–48)

The son of Casimir IV. A great patron of the Renaissance. His court was divided by factions and from 1518 the Protestant Reformation raised new troubles. In a war with Russia he lost Smolensk (1514), but gained E Prussia (1525) and Moldavia (1531). He was succeeded by his son, Sigismund II Augustus.

Sigismund II Augustus (1520–72)
King of Poland (1548–72)

The son of Sigismund I. In 1530 he was crowned co-ruler with his father, whom he later succeeded. His reign saw the wide spread of Protestantism, the union of Poland and Lithuania, and the conquest of Livonia.

Sigismund III Vasa (1561–1632)
King of Poland (1587–1632) and Sweden (1592–99)

The Catholic son of Johan III of Sweden, and nephew of Sigismund II Augustus of Poland. Deposed in Sweden by his Protestant uncle, Charles IX (1599) he made several unsuccessful attempts to regain his crown. He also invaded Russia (1609–12), fought in Moldavia against Ottoman forces (1617–21), and lost Livonia in a long war with Gustavus II of Sweden (1621–9). He was succeeded in Poland by his son, Ladislas IV Vasa.

Sigurd I, the Crusader (c.1090–1130)
King of Norway (1103–30)

The youngest of the three sons of Magnus III, whom he succeeded, ruling jointly with his brothers until their deaths (1015 and 1022). He did much to strengthen the church, and was the first Scandinavian king to take part in the Crusades (1107–11).

Stanisław I or Stanisław Leszczyński (1677–1766)
King of Poland (1704–9, 1733–5)

He was deposed in 1709 by Peter the Great to make room for Augustus II. Re-elected in 1733, he lost the War of the Polish Succession and formally abdicated in 1736.

Stanisław II (August) Poniatowski (1732–98)
King of Poland (1764–95)

A favourite of the future empress, Catherine II of Russia, through whose influence he was elected king. His reign saw the first, second and third partitions of Poland (1772, 1793, 1795), in which Poland as an independent state was wiped from the face of the map, its territories being divided between Russia, Austria and Prussia. In 1795 the Polish monarchy was at an end and Stanisław resigned his crown.

Stephen (c.1090–1154)
King of England (1135–54)

The son of Stephen, Count of Blois, and Adela, the daughter of William the Conqueror. Although he had sworn to accept Henry I's daughter, Empress Matilda, as queen, on Henry's death he seized the English Crown and was also recognized as Duke of Normandy. Though captured at the battle of Lincoln (Feb 1141), he was released nine months later after Matilda's supporters had been routed at Winchester. Meanwhile David I of Scotland had annexed the N English counties and by 1145 Matilda's husband, Geoffrey of Anjou, had conquered Normandy. Stephen was also repeatedly challenged by baronial rebellions, and after 18 years of conflict, he was forced in 1153 to accept Matilda's son, the future Henry II, as his lawful successor. He was the last Norman king of England.

Stephen I (997–1038)
King of Hungary

The first king of Hungary, he formed a kingdom out of Pannonia and Dacia, organized the Christian Church, and introduced many social and economic reforms. Pope Sylvester II gave him the title of 'Apostolic King' and, according to tradition, St Stephen's Crown, which is now a Hungarian national treasure. Canonized in 1083, he is the patron saint of Hungary.

Stephen Bathory (1533–86)
King of Poland (1575–86)

He defeated an attempted Russian invasion of Livonia under Ivan the Terrible and successfully reached a tolerant solution to the religious divisions brought about by the Reformation in Poland.

Sverrir Sigurdsson, the Usurper (c.1150–1202)
King of Norway (1184–1202)

Claiming to be the illegitimate son of King Sigurd Haraldsson, 'the Mouth', he deposed and killed Magnus V in 1184. He turned out to be one of Norway's greatest kings, strengthening the crown against both church and nobles. He commissioned one of the first Icelandic Sagas — a biography of himself, *Sverris saga*.

Sweyn I, Forkbeard (d.1014)
King of Denmark (987–1014) and England (1013–14)

The son of Harold Blue-tooth, and the father of Canute. He first attacked England in 994, and during his final campaign in 1013, conquered the whole country and was recognized as king, while Ethelred the Unready withdrew to exile in Normandy.

Sweyn II (d.1074)
King of Denmark (1047–74)

A nephew of Canute the Great. He was appointed regent of Denmark in 1045 by Magnus I of Norway and Denmark, and proclaimed himself king when Magnus died. His claim was contested by Harold III of Norway, who waged war against Sweyn until 1064. In 1069 Sweyn's army descended on the north of England and captured York, but withdrew the following year. He was succeeded by five of his sons in turn.

t

Tarquinius Priscus
The fifth king of Rome (616–578 BC)

Of Etruscan origin, he is said to have modified the constitution, and to have begun the building of a wall around the city and the Circus Maximus (the largest arena in Rome).

Tarquinius Superbus, the Proud (6c BC)
The seventh king of Rome (534–510 BC)

Possibly of Etruscan extraction. His overthrow marked the end of monarchy in Rome, and the beginning of the Republic.

Theodore or Baron von Neuhoff (1686–1756)
King of Corsica (1736)

The son of a Westphalian noble. In 1736, he led a Corsican rising against the Genoese. He was elected king, but after seven months left to obtain foreign aid. He attempted unsuccessfully to return in 1738 and in 1743.

Theodoric I (d.451 AD)
King of the Visigoths (AD 418–451)

The son of Alaric I. He attacked the Romans in Gaul, besieged Narbonne, and defeated the Roman army at Toulouse (AD 439). On the invasion of Attila in AD 451, he joined with the Romans to drive back the Huns, but was killed in battle.

Theodoric II (d.466 AD)
King of the Visigoths (AD 453–66)

The son of Theodoric I, and brother of Thorismund — whom he assassinated. He installed Eparchius Avitus as Roman Emperor, but on Avitus's abdication in AD 456, he broke the friendship with Rome and besieged Arles. In AD 462 he made another attempt on Gaul, but was defeated near Orléans (AD 464). He was murdered in AD 466 by his brother Euric, who succeeded him.

Theodoric, the Great (AD 455–526)
King of the Ostrogoths (AD 471–526)

He invaded Italy in AD 489 and defeated the barbarian ruler, Odoacer. His long reign was a time of peace and prosperity for Italy, where the Goths and the Romans continued as distinct nations, each with its own laws.

Tigranes I, the Great (d. after 56 BC)
King of Armenia

He was set on the throne by Parthian troops c.94 BC. Left undisturbed owing to a Roman agreement with the Parthians, he made many conquests but was eventually forced to surrendered to Pompey (66 BC), from this time ruling over Armenia only.

U

Ulrika Eleonora (1688–1741)
Queen of Sweden (1719–20)

The younger sister of Charles XII, whom she succeeded. However, the so-called 'Era of Liberty' (1718–71), saw the abolition of royal absolutism and Ulrika was so displeased that she abdicated in 1720 in favour of her husband, Prince Frederick of Hesse, who ascended the throne as Frederick I.

Umberto I (1844–1900)
King of Italy (1878–1900)

He fought in a war against Austria (1866) and, after he came to the throne, brought Italy into the Triple Alliance with Germany and Austria (1882). He supported Italian colonialism in Africa, but his popularity declined after Italy's defeat by the Ethiopians at Adowa (1896), and he was assassinated in Monza.

Umberto II (1904–83)
King of Italy (1946)

He succeeded to the throne on the abdication of his father, Victor Emmanuel III, but he too abdicated a month later, after a national referendum had declared for a republic.

Victor Emmanuel I (1759–1824)
King of Sardinia (1802–21)

His oppressive rule led to a revolt in 1821, when he abdicated in favour of his brother, Charles Felix.

Victor Emmanuel II (1820–78)
King of Italy (1861–78)

As King of Sardinia from 1849, he appointed Conte Camillo Cavour as his Chief Minister (1852). His war against Austria (1859) brought him Lombardy, and in 1860 Modena, Parma, the Romagna, and Tuscany were peacefully annexed. Sicily and Naples were added by Giuseppe Garibaldi, and Savoy and Nice were surrendered to France. Proclaimed king at Turin, he supported Prussia in the Austro-Prussian War (1866), and after the fall of the French Empire (1870) he annexed Rome.

Victor Emmanuel III (1869–1947)
King of Italy (1900–46)

Initially a constitutional monarch, he defied his parliament by bringing Italy into World War I on the side of the Allies (1915), and by offering Mussolini the premiership (1922). Reduced to a figurehead by the Fascist government, he played an important part in bringing down Mussolini (1943), but his association with fascism had tainted him forever and he abdicated in 1946.

Victoria (Alexandrina) (1819–1901)
Queen of Great Britain (from 1837) and Ireland and
Empress of India (from 1876)

The only child of George III's fourth son, Edward, and Victoria Maria Louisa of Saxe-Coburg . She understood constitutional principles and the extent of her own authority, which she first exercised in 1839 on the fall of Melbourne's government, triggering the 'Bedchamber Crisis' and prolonging Melbourne's ministry until 1841. In 1840 she married Prince Albert of Saxe-Coburg and Gotha, and they had four sons and five daughters. She was strongly influenced by her husband and after his death (1861) withdrew from public life. Her seclusion caused her to fall from public favour, but with her recognition as Empress of India, and the celebratory golden (1887) and diamond (1897) jubilees, her popularity and prestige were restored. She had strong preferences for certain (more conservative) Prime Ministers (notably Melbourne and Benjamin Disraeli) over others (notably Peel and Gladstone), but on Albert's advice stayed within the framework of the constitution. At various points in her long reign she exercised some influence over foreign affairs, and the marriages of her children had important diplomatic, as well as dynastic, implications in Europe. She was succeeded by her son, Edward VII.

> We are not amused.
>
> *1900 Attrib, 20 Jan*

Vortigern (5c)
Semi-legendary British king

After the final Roman withdrawal from Britain (AD 409), he is said to have recruited Germanic mercenaries led by Hengist and Horsa to help fight off the Picts. Tradition has it that when these troops revolted, they started the Germanic conquests and settlements in England.

ω

Waldemar I, the Great (1131–82)
King of Denmark (1157–82)

The son of King Canute Lavard, he emerged victorious from 30 years of civil war to give Denmark a period of prosperity and expansion. He was succeeded by his eldest son, Canute VI.

Wenceslas I, St ('Good King Wenceslas') (c.903–35)
Duke and patron of Bohemia (c.924–35)

He received a Christian education from his grandmother and, after the death of his father (c.924), encouraged the spread of Christianity in Bohemia via German missionary priests. This antagonized his non-Christian opponents, among them his pagan mother Dragomir. When he placed the duchy under the protection of the German king, Henry the Fowler, his enemies were sufficiently incensed to murder him. His brother Boleslaw killed him on his way to mass, probably at their mother's instigation. Almost immediately, he became the patron saint of Bohemia and Czechoslovakia.

Wenceslas IV (1361–1419)
Holy Roman Emperor and King of Germany (1378–1400) and King of Bohemia (1378–1419)

The son of Emperor Charles IV, whom he succeeded. An ineffective ruler who allowed Germany to slide into anarchy, he was deposed as emperor in 1400.

Wilhelmina (Helena Pauline Maria) (1880–1962)
Queen of the Netherlands (1890–1948)

She succeeded her father William III at the age of 10, and her mother acted as regent until 1898. An upholder of constitutional monarchy, she won the admiration of her people, particularly during World War II, when she steadfastly encouraged Dutch resistance to the German occupation, though she herself had to seek refuge in Britain. She abdicated in favour of her daughter Juliana.

William I, the Conqueror (c.1028–87)
Duke of Normandy (1035–87) and King of England (1066–87)

The illegitimate son of Duke Robert of Normandy. Edward the Confessor is thought to have named him as his successor in 1051, and so when Harold Godwin took the throne as Harold II, William invaded, defeated and killed Harold at the battle of Hastings, and was crowned king. This military conquest was backed by aristocratic colonization — by the time of the Domesday Book (1086), the Anglo-Saxon leaders south of the Tees had been almost entirely replaced by a new ruling class of Normans, Bretons, and Flemings, who were loyal to William.

> This William of whom we speak was a very wise man, and very powerful and more worshipful and stronger than any predecessor of his had been.
>
> *1087* Anglo-Saxon Chronicle

William II or William Rufus (c.1056–1100)
King of England (1087–1100)

The second surviving son of William the Conqueror. He fought to recover Normandy from his elder brother Robert Curthose, and from 1096, when Robert departed on the First Crusade, William ruled the duchy. He also led expeditions to Wales (1095, 1097); conquered Carlisle and the surrounding district (1092); and after the death of Malcolm Canmore, exercised some control in Scottish affairs. He exploited his rights over the Church and the nobility, and quarrelled with Anselm, Archbishop of Canterbury. His death by an arrow while hunting was supposed by some to have been a murder ordered by his younger brother, who succeeded him as Henry I.

William III or William of Orange (1650–1702)
Stadtholder of the United Provinces (from 1672) and King of Great Britain (from 1689)

The son of Mary (the eldest daughter of Charles I of England) and William II of Orange. In 1677 he married Mary, the daughter of James II. Invited to Britain to protect the Protestant religion, he landed at Torbay in 1688 with an English and Dutch army, and forced the Catholic James II to flee. William and Mary were proclaimed joint rulers early the following year. He defeated James's supporters at Killiecrankie (1689) and at the Boyne (1690), then concentrated on the War of the Grand Alliance against France (1689–97), in which he was eventually successful. After surviving several assassination plots, he died childless, and the Crown passed to Mary's sister Anne.

> His strength lay rather in a true discerning and a sound judgment than in imagination or invention.
>
> *Gilbert Burnet*, History of my own Time

William IV, the Sailor King (1765–1837)
King of Great Britain and Ireland, and King of Hanover (1830–7)

The third son of George III and brother of George IV, whom he succeeded. He entered the navy in 1779, becoming Admiral in 1811, and Lord High Admiral in 1827–8. Believed to have been a Whig until his accession, as king he revealed Tory sympathies and did his best to prevent the passing of the first Reform Act (1832). He was the last monarch to dismiss a ministry with a parliamentary majority when he sacked the Whig Melbourne (1834) and invited the Tories to form a government. His niece succeeded him as Queen Victoria.

> . . . so excessively rude that there was no bearing it.
>
> *1783 Letter from the Bishop of Osnaburgh to the Prince of Wales*

William I, the Lion (c.1142–1214)
King of Scots (1165–1214)

The brother and successor of Malcolm IV. In 1173–4 he invaded Northumberland during the rebellion against Henry II, but was captured at Alnwick, and by the Treaty of Falaise (1174) recognized Henry as the feudal superior of Scotland. He nevertheless strengthened his kingdom, and in 1192 Celestine III declared the Scottish Church free of all external authority save the pope's. He was succeeded by his son, Alexander II.

William I or Wilhelm (1797–1888)
King of Prussia (1861–88) and first German Emperor (1871–88)

The second son of Frederick-William III. His use of force during the 1848 revolution made him unpopular, and he had to leave Prussia temporarily for London. As king, he strengthened the monarchy; Bismarck was placed at the head of the ministry, with Albert von

Roon as War Minister. He was victorious against Denmark (1864), Austria (1866), and France in 1871, when he was proclaimed Emperor of Germany. The rapid rise of socialism in Germany led him to take severely repressive measures. He survived several assassination attempts.

William II or Wilhelm (1859–1941)
German Emperor and King of Prussia (1888–1918)

The eldest son of Frederick III and grandson of William I. He dismissed Bismarck (1890), and began a long period of personal rule. Aggressive in international affairs, he pledged full support to Austria–Hungary after the assassination of Archduke Francis Ferdinand in Sarajevo (1914). During World War I he became a mere figurehead, and when the German armies collapsed, and US President Wilson refused to negotiate while he remained in power, he abdicated, fled the country, and settled in the Netherlands.

> We fought for our place in the sun and won it. Our future is on the water.
>
> *1901 Speech, Elbe regatta, Jun*

Z

Zog I (1895–1961)
King of the Albanians (1928–39)

Originally Ahmed Bey Zogu, the son of a highland tribal chieftain.
When Albania declared its independence in 1912, Zog took a blood
oath to defend it. In 1922 he formed a republican government and in
1928 proclaimed himself king. When, at Easter 1939, Albania was
annexed by the Italians, Zog was forced into exile. His son, Leka,
was proclaimed king in exile on his father's death.

Appendices

Heads of European
Royal Houses

NB: many of the following may have renounced their right of succession.

Austria–Hungary
Otto von Habsburg-Lothringen (1912–   )

The eldest son of Charles I, last emperor of Austria, and Princess Zita of Parma. He renounced his right of succession. In 1951 he married Regina of Saxe-Meiningen and their eldest son is Karl.

Bulgaria
Simeon II (1937–   )

Exiled king. The son of Boris III and Princess Giovanna of Savoy (daughter of Victor Emmanuel III). In 1962 he married Margarita Gomez Acebo y Cejuela.

France — Imperial House of Napoleon
Charles Jerome Victor Napoleon (1950–   )

The son of Louis, Prince Napoleon, and Alix, daughter of Count Alberic de Foresta. He is a descendant of Jérôme, King of Westphalia. In 1978 he married Beatrice of Bourbon-Sicily.

France—Royal House of Bourbon-Orléans
Henri, Count of Clermont (1933–   )

The son of Henri, Count of Paris, and Isabelle, daughter of Prince Pedro of Orléans and Braganza. A descendant of Philippe Egalité. In 1957 he married Duchess Maria-Theresa of Württemberg. His eldest son, Francis-Henri, was born in 1961.

Greece
Constantine II (1940–   )

Exiled king. The son of Paul I and Princess Fredericka of Brunswick. In 1964 he married Princess Anne Marie of Denmark. His son Paul, Duke of Sparta, was born in 1967.

Italy
Victor Emmanuel, Prince of Savoy and Naples (1937–   )

The son of Umberto II and Princess Marie Joseph, daughter of Albert I, King of the Belgians. In 1971 he married Marina Doria. His son Emmanuel Philiberto was born in 1972.

Portugal
Edward (Duarte), Duke of Braganza (1945–   )

The great-grandson of Miguel I; and son of Edward, Duke of Braganza, and Maria-Francisca, daughter of Prince Pedro of Orléans and Braganza.

Heads of European Royal Houses

Prussia

Claimants would be descendants of Grand Duchess Kira Kirillovna of Russia and Louis Ferdinand, Prince of Prussia (1907–94), himself the grandson of William II of Prussia and Augusta of Schleswig-Holstein. These are: Frederick William (1939–   ) who renounced his right of succession in 1966; Michael (1940–   ) who renounced his right of succession in 1966; Louis Ferdinand (1944–77) who did not renounce his right of succession and was seen as a possible claimant; and Christian Sigismund (1946–   ). Louis Ferdinand's son, George Frederick, was born in 1976.

Romania
Michael (1921–   )

Exiled king. The son of Carol II. He abdicated in 1947. In 1948 he married Anne of Bourbon-Parma. They have five daughters.

Russia
Vladimir, Grand Duke of Russia (1917–92)

The great-grandson of Alexander II and Marie of Hesse. He married Leonida of Bagration-Mukhianski. On his death his grandson George — son of Vladimir's daughter Maria and Prince Francis William of Prussia — became the claimant.

Yugoslavia
Crown Prince Alexander (1945–   )

The son of the exiled King of Yugoslavia, Peter II, and Alexandra (daughter of Alex I, King of the Hellenes). In 1972 he married Maria de Gloria, daughter of Prince Pedro of Orléans and Braganza. They have three sons.

DESCENDANTS OF THE HOUSE OF STUART

Scotland
Prince Michael Stewart of Albany (1958–   )

Seventh generation descendant of Prince Charles Edward Louis Philip Casimir Stuart (1720–88), known as 'Bonnie Prince Charlie', himself the elder son of James Francis Stuart (1688–1766). He aspires to become a constitutional monarch of an independent Scotland.

United Kingdom
Albrecht Luitpold Ferdinand Michael von Bayern, Duke of Bavaria (1905–   )

A descendant of Henrietta Anne (1644–70), daughter of Charles I and sister to Charles II. He has four children: twin daughters Marie Gabriele and Marie Charlotte (1931–   ); his heir, Franz (1933–   ); and a second son, Max Emanuel (1937–   ).

Monarchic Dynasties
and Emperors

HOUSE OF ATHOLL

Kings and Queens of Scotland

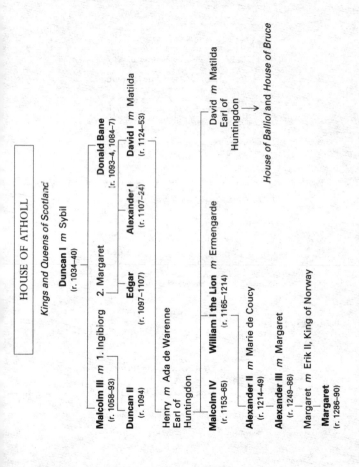

Duncan I *m* Sybil
(r. 1034–40)

Malcolm III *m* 1. Ingibiorg   2. Margaret   **Donald Bane**   **David I** *m* Matilda
(r. 1058–93)   [r. 1093–4, 1084–7]   (r. 1124–53)

Duncan II   **Edgar**   **Alexander I**
(r. 1094)   (r. 1097–1107)   (r. 1107–24)

Henry *m* Ada de Warenne   David *m* Matilda
Earl of   Earl of
Huntingdon   Huntingdon

William I the Lion *m* Ermengarde   *House of Balliol* and *House of Bruce*
(r. 1165–1214)

Malcolm IV
(r. 1153–65)

Alexander II *m* Marie de Coucy
(r. 1214–49)

Alexander III *m* Margaret
(r. 1249–86)

Margaret *m* Erik II, King of Norway

Margaret
(r. 1286–90)

133

HOUSE OF BALLIOL

Kings of Scotland

John Balliol *m* Devorguilla
|
John *m* Isabel de Warenne
(r. 1292–6)
|
Edward   (rival claimant to the
(r. 1332–56)   throne of David II)

HOUSE OF BRUCE

Kings of Scotland

Robert I *m* 1. Isabella of Mar   2. Elizabeth de Burgh
(r. 1306–29)

Marjorie Bruce *m* Walter,   **David II**
6th High Steward   (r. 1329–71)
of Scotland

↓

House of Stuart

HOUSE OF BLOIS

Kings of England

Adela *m* Stephen Count of Blois
Stephen
(r. 1135–54)

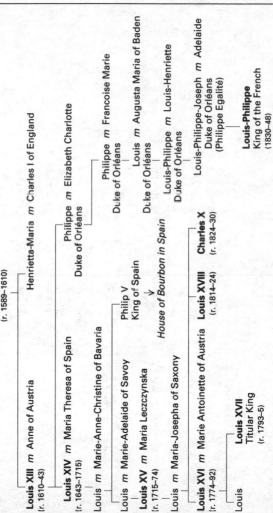

HOUSE OF BOURBON IN FRANCE

Henry IV *m* Marie de Medici
(r. 1589–1610)

Henrietta-Maria *m* Charles I of England

Philippe *m* Elizabeth Charlotte
Duke of Orléans

Philippe *m* Francoise Marie
Duke of Orléans

Louis *m* Augusta Maria of Baden
Duke of Orléans

Louis-Philippe *m* Louis-Henriette
Duke of Orléans

Louis-Philippe-Joseph *m* Adelaide
Duke of Orléans
(Philippe Egalité)

Louis-Philippe
King of the French
(1830–48)

Louis XIII *m* Anne of Austria
(r. 1610–43)

Louis XIV *m* Maria Theresa of Spain
(r. 1643–1715)

Louis *m* Marie-Anne-Christine of Bavaria

Philip V
King of Spain

House of Bourbon in Spain

Louis XV *m* Maria Leczczynska
(r. 1715–74)

Louis *m* Marie-Adelaide of Savoy

Louis XVIII
(r. 1814–24)

Charles X
(r. 1824–30)

Louis *m* Maria-Josepha of Saxony

Louis XVI *m* Marie Antoinette of Austria
(r. 1774–92)

Louis

Louis XVII
Titular King
(r. 1793–5)

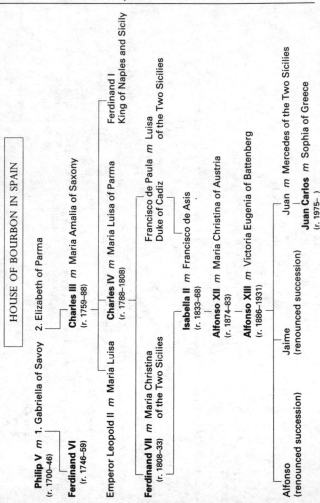

House of Bourbon in Spain

HOUSE OF BOURBON IN SPAIN

Philip V *m* 1. Gabriella of Savoy 2. Elizabeth of Parma
(r. 1700–46)

Ferdinand VI
(r. 1746–59)

Charles III *m* Maria Amalia of Saxony
(r. 1759–88)

Emperor Leopold II *m* Maria Luisa

Charles IV *m* Maria Luisa of Parma
(r. 1788–1808)

Ferdinand I
King of Naples and Sicily

Ferdinand VII *m* Maria Christina
(r. 1808–33) of the Two Sicilies

Francisco de Paula *m* Luisa of the Two Sicilies
Duke of Cadiz

Isabella II *m* Francisco de Asis
(r. 1833–68)

Alfonso XII *m* Maria Christina of Austria
(r. 1874–83)

Alfonso XIII *m* Victoria Eugenia of Battenberg
(r. 1886–1931)

Alfonso
(renounced succession)

Jaime
(renounced succession)

Juan *m* Mercedes of the Two Sicilies

Juan Carlos *m* Sophia of Greece
(r. 1975–)

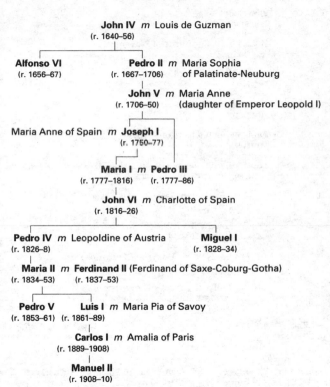

HOUSE OF BRAGANZA

Kings of Portugal

John IV *m* Louis de Guzman
(r. 1640–56)

Alfonso VI **Pedro II** *m* Maria Sophia
(r. 1656–67) (r. 1667–1706) of Palatinate-Neuburg

John V *m* Maria Anne
(r. 1706–50) (daughter of Emperor Leopold I)

Maria Anne of Spain *m* **Joseph I**
(r. 1750–77)

Maria I *m* Pedro III
(r. 1777–1816) (r. 1777–86)

John VI *m* Charlotte of Spain
(r. 1816–26)

Pedro IV *m* Leopoldine of Austria **Miguel I**
(r. 1826–8)   (r. 1828–34)

Maria II *m* Ferdinand II (Ferdinand of Saxe-Coburg-Gotha)
(r. 1834–53) (r. 1837–53)

Pedro V **Luis I** *m* Maria Pia of Savoy
(r. 1853–61) (r. 1861–89)

Carlos I *m* Amalia of Paris
(r. 1889–1908)

Manuel II
(r. 1908–10)

HOUSE OF CAPET

Kings of France

Hugh Capet
(r. 987–96)

Robert II *m* Constance of Provence
(r. 996–1031)

Henry I *m* Anne of Kiev
(r. 1031–60)

Philip I *m* Bertha
(r. 1067–1108)

Louis VI *m* Adelaide of Savoy
(r. 1108–37)

Louis VII *m* 1. Eleanor of Aquitaine *m* Henry II of England
(r. 1137–80)   2. Adela of Champagne

Philip II *m* Isabella of Hainault
(r. 1180–1223)

Louis VIII *m* Blanche of Castile
(r. 1223–6)

Louis IX *m* Margaret of Provence
(r. 1226–70)

Philip III *m* Isabella of Aragon
(r. 1270–85)

Philip IV *m* Joanna of Navarre   Charles *m* Margaret
(r. 1285–1314)   Count of Valois   of Anjou

Louis X *m* 1. Margaret   2. Clementia   **Philip V**   **Charles IV**
(r. 1314–16)   of Burgundy   of Hungary   (r. 1316–22)   (r. 1322–8)

Joanna,   John I
Queen of   (r. 1316)
Navarre

Isabella *m* Edward II
of England

*House of
Valois*

138

DANISH KINGS OF ENGLAND

Sweyn *m* Gunhild
(r. 1013–14)

Canute *m* 1. Aelfgifu of   2. Emma of Normandy
(r. 1016–35)   Northampton   (widow of Ethelred II)

   Harold I Harefoot   **Hardicanute**
   (r. 1037–40)   (r. 1040–2)

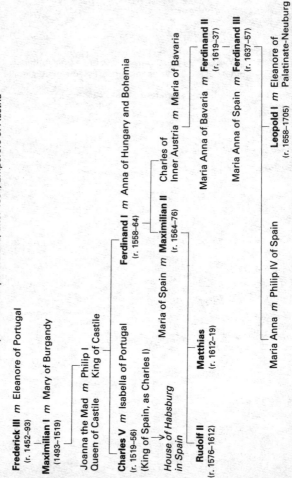

House of Habsburg

HOUSE OF HABSBURG

Holy Roman Emperors and, after 1804, Emperors of Austria

Frederick III *m* Eleanore of Portugal
(r. 1452–93)

Maximilian I *m* Mary of Burgandy
(1493–1519)

Joanna the Mad *m* Philip I
King of Castile
Queen of Castile

Charles V *m* Isabella of Portugal
(r. 1519–56)
(King of Spain, as Charles I)

→ *House of Habsburg in Spain*

Rudolf II
(r. 1576–1612)

Matthias
(r. 1612–19)

Ferdinand I *m* Anna of Hungary and Bohemia
(r. 1558–64)

Maria of Spain *m* **Maximilian II**
(r. 1564–76)

Charles of Inner Austria *m* Maria of Bavaria

Maria Anna of Bavaria *m* **Ferdinand II**
(r. 1619–37)

Maria Anna of Spain *m* **Ferdinand III**
(r. 1637–57)

Maria Anna *m* Philip IV of Spain

Leopold I *m* Eleanore of Palatinate-Neuburg
(r. 1658–1705)

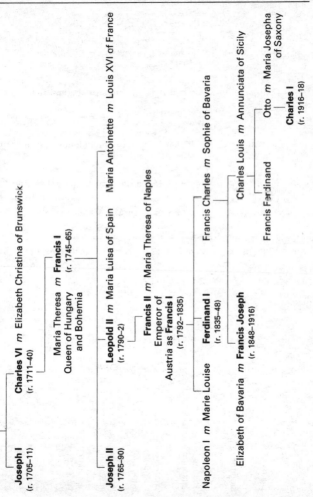

Joseph I
(r. 1705–11)

Charles VI _m_ Elizabeth Christina of Brunswick
(r. 1711–40)

Maria Theresa _m_ Francis I
Queen of Hungary   (r. 1745–65)
and Bohemia

Joseph II
(r. 1765–90)

Leopold II _m_ Maria Luisa of Spain
(r. 1790–2)

Maria Antoinette _m_ Louis XVI of France

Francis II _m_ Maria Theresa of Naples
Emperor of
Austria as Francis I
(r. 1792–1835)

Napoleon I _m_ Marie Louise

Ferdinand I
(r. 1835–48)

Francis Charles _m_ Sophie of Bavaria

Elizabeth of Bavaria _m_ Francis Joseph
(r. 1848–1916)

Charles Louis _m_ Annunciata of Sicily

Francis Ferdinand

Otto _m_ Maria Josepha
of Saxony

Charles I
(r. 1916–18)

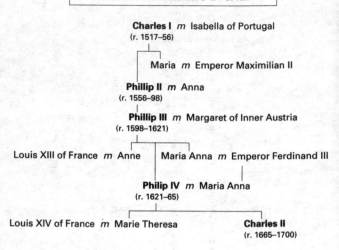

HOUSE OF HABSBURG IN SPAIN

Charles I *m* Isabella of Portugal
(r. 1517–56)

Maria *m* Emperor Maximilian II

Phillip II *m* Anna
(r. 1556–98)

Phillip III *m* Margaret of Inner Austria
(r. 1598–1621)

Louis XIII of France *m* Anne   Maria Anna *m* Emperor Ferdinand III

Philip IV *m* Maria Anna
(r. 1621–65)

Louis XIV of France *m* Marie Theresa   **Charles II**
(r. 1665–1700)

HOUSE OF HANOVER

Kings of Great Britain and Ireland

Elizabeth *m* Frederick V
      Elector palatine of the Rhine

Sophia *m* Ernest Augustus
      Elector of Hanover

George I *m* Dorothea of Zell
(r. 1714–27)

George II *m* Caroline of Ansbach
(r. 1727–60)

Frederick Louis *m* Augusta of Saxe-Gotha
Prince of Wales

George III *m* Charlotte Sophia
(r. 1760–1820)

Edward *m* Victoria Mary Louise Duke of Kent	**George IV** (r. 1820–30)	**William IV** (r. 1830–7)

↓

House of Saxe-Coburg-Gotha

HOHENSTAUFEN DYNASTY

Holy Roman Emperors

Frederick I of Swabia *m* Agnes (daughter of Emperor Henry IV)

Conrad III   Frederick II of Swabia *m* Judith of Bavaria
(r. 1138–52)

               Frederick I *m* Beatrix of Burgundy
               (r. 1152–90)

Constance of Sicily *m* **Henry VI**   **Philip of Swabia**
             (r. 1191–7)   (r. 1198–1208)

Frederick II *m* Isabella of Brienne
(r. 1220–50)

Conrad IV
(r. 1250–4)

HOHENZOLLERN DYNASTY

Kings of Prussia and German Emperors

Frederick-William I m Louise Henriette of Orange
Elector of Brandenburg
|
Frederick I m Sophia Charlotte (sister of George I of Britain)
(r. 1701–13)
|
Frederick-William I m Sophia Dorothea (daughter of George I of Britain)
(r. 1713–40)
|
┌─────────────────────────┬──────────────────────────┐
| |
Frederick II   Louise Ulrika m Adolf Frederick of Sweden   Augustus William m Louise of Brunswick
(r. 1740–86) |
                                                      Frederick-William II m Frederica of Hesse-Darmstadt
                                                      (r. 1786–97)
                                                      |
                                                      Frederick-William III m Louisa of Mecklenburg-Strelitz
                                                      (r. 1797–1840)
                                                      |
                                          ┌───────────┴───────────┐
                                          | |
                              Frederick-William IV   **William I** m Augusta of Saxe-Weimar
                              (r. 1840–61)   (r. 1861–88)
                                                          |
                                                          Frederick III m Victoria (daughter of Victoria of Great Britain)
                                                          (r. 1888)
                                                          |
                                                          William II
                                                          (r. 1888–1918)

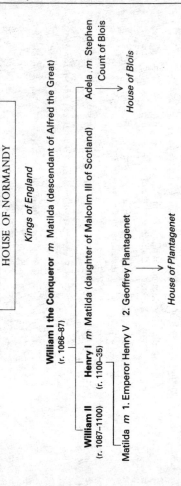

HOUSE OF NORMANDY

Kings of England

William I the Conqueror *m* Matilda (descendant of Alfred the Great)
(r. 1066–87)

Adela . *m* Stephen Count of Blois

House of Blois

William II **Henry I** *m* Matilda (daughter of Malcolm III of Scotland)
(r. 1087–1100) (r. 1100–35)

Matilda *m* 1. Emperor Henry V 2. Geoffrey Plantagenet

House of Plantagenet

HOUSE OF PLANTAGENET

Kings of England

Henry II m Eleanor of Aquitaine
(r. 1154–89)

Richard I
(r. 1189–99)

John m Isabella of Angoulême
(r. 1199–1216)

Henry III m Eleanor of Provence
(r. 1216–72)

Edward I m Eleanor of Castile   Edmund Crouchback
(r. 1272–1307)

Edward II m Isabella of France
(r. 1307–27)

Edward III m Phillipa of Hainault
(r. 1327–77)

Edward the Black Prince m Joan
(granddaughter of Edward II)

Richard II
(r. 1377–99)

Edmund Duke of York → *House of York*

John of Gaunt → *House of Lancaster*

HOUSE OF SAVOY

Kings of Sardinia and, after 1861, of Italy

Victor Amadeus II *m* Anna of Orléans
(r. 1620–1730)

Charles Emmanuel III *m* Polyxena of Rheinfels-Rottenberg
(r. 1730–73)

Victor Amadeus III *m* Mary of Spain
(r. 1773–96)

Charles Emmanuel IV   **Victor Emmanuel I**   **Charles Felix**
(r. 1796–1802)   (r. 1802–21)   (r. 1821–31)

Charles Albert *m* Theresa of Tuscany
(descendant of
Charles Emmanuel I)
(r. 1831–49)

Victor Emmanuel II *m* Adelaide of Austria
(r. 1849–78)

Umberto I *m* Margherita of Savoy   **Amadeus I**
(r. 1878–1900)   (his cousin)   King of Spain
                                                (r. 1870–3)
Victor Emmanuel III *m* Helen of Montenegro
(r. 1900–46)

Umberto II
(r. 1946)

HOUSE OF SAXE-COBURG-GOTHA

*Kings and Queens of Great Britain and,
to 1922, of Ireland (thereafter, of
Northern Ireland)*

Victoria *m* Albert
(r. 1837–1901)   Prince of Saxe-Coburg-Gotha

Edward VII *m* Alexandra of Denmark
(r. 1901–10)

George V *m* Mary of Teck
(r. 1910–36)

House of Windsor*

*name changed from Saxe-Coburg Gotha in 1917

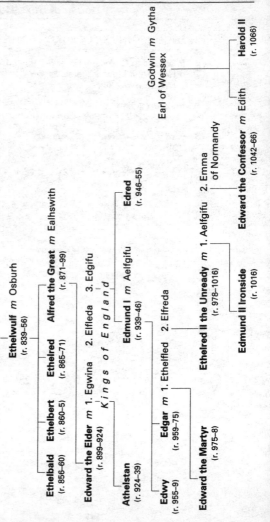

HOUSE OF STUART

Kings and Queens of Scotland

Robert II *m* Elizabeth Mure
(r. 1371–90)

Robert III *m* Annabella Drummond
(r. 1390–1406)

James I *m* Joan Beaufort
(r. 1406–37)

James II *m* Mary of Gueldres
(r. 1437–60)

James III *m* Margaret of Denmark
(r. 1460–88)

James IV *m* Margaret Tudor
(r. 1488–1513)   (daughter of Henry VII)

James V *m* Mary of Guise
(r. 1513–42)

Mary, Queen of Scots *m* Henry, Lord Darnley
(r. 1542–67)

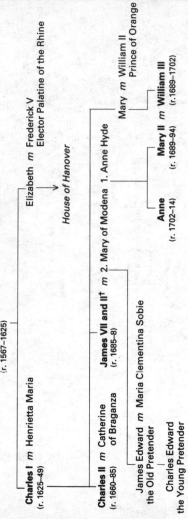
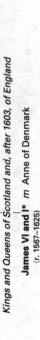

Kings and Queens of Scotland and, after 1603, of England

James VI and I* *m* Anne of Denmark
(r. 1567–1625)

Elizabeth *m* Frederick V
Elector Palatine of the Rhine

→ *House of Hanover*

Mary *m* William II
Prince of Orange

Charles I *m* Henrietta Maria
(r. 1625–49)

Charles II *m* Catherine
(r. 1660–85)   of Braganza

James VII and II† *m* 2. Mary of Modena   1. Anne Hyde
(r. 1685–8)

James Edward *m* Maria Clementina Sobie
the Old Pretender

Charles Edward
the Young Pretender

Anne
(r. 1702–14)

Mary II *m* **William III**
(r. 1689–94)   (r. 1689–1702)

*James VI of Scotland from 1567 and
James I of England from 1603

†James VII of Scotland and
James II of England

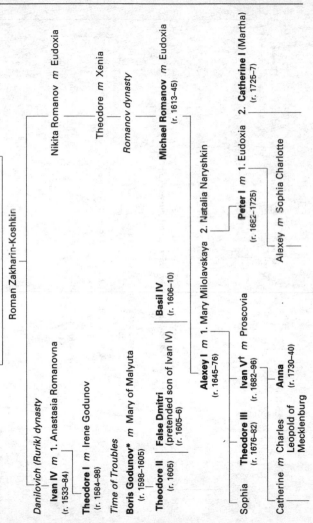

TSARS OF RUSSIA

Roman Zakharin-Koshkin

Danilovich (Rurik dynasty)

Ivan IV *m* 1. Anastasia Romanovna
(r. 1533–84)

Theodore I *m* Irene Godunov
(r. 1584–98)

Time of Troubles

Boris Godunov* *m* Mary of Malyuta
(r. 1598–1605)

Theodore II | False Dmitri
(r. 1605) | (pretended son of Ivan IV)
| (r. 1605–6)

Basil IV
(r. 1606–10)

Nikita Romanov *m* Eudoxia

Theodore *m* Xenia

Romanov dynasty

Michael Romanov *m* Eudoxia
(r. 1613–45)

Alexey I *m* 1. Mary Milolavskaya   2. Natalia Naryshkin
(r. 1645–76)

Peter I *m* 1. Eudoxia
(r. 1682–1725)

Alexey *m* Sophia Charlotte

Sophia

Theodore III
(r. 1676–82)

Ivan V† *m* Proscovia
(r. 1682–96)

Anna
(r. 1730–40)

Catherine *m* Charles Leopold of Mecklenburg

Catherine I (Martha)
2. Catherine I
(r. 1725–7)

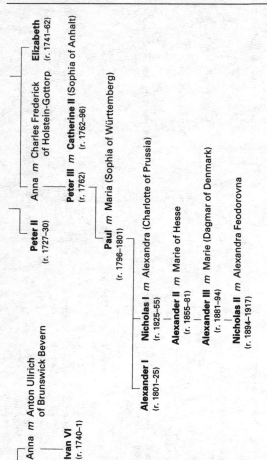

Elizabeth (r. 1741–62)

Anna *m* Charles Frederick of Holstein-Gottorp

Peter II (r. 1727–30)

Peter III *m* Maria (Sophia of Anhalt) (r. 1762) Catherine II (Sophia of Anhalt) (r. 1762–96)

Paul *m* Maria (Sophia of Württemberg) (r. 1796–1801)

Nicholas I *m* Alexandra (Charlotte of Prussia) (r. 1825–55)

Alexander II *m* Marie of Hesse (r. 1855–81)

Alexander III *m* Marie (Dagmar of Denmark) (r. 1881–94)

Nicholas II *m* Alexandra Feodorovna (r. 1894–1917)

Alexander I (r. 1801–25)

Anna *m* Anton Ullrich of Brunswick Bevern

Ivan VI (r. 1740–1)

154

*brother of Irene Godunov
†co-ruler with Peter I

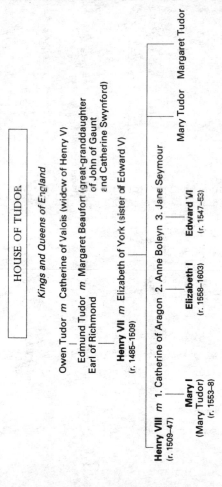

HOUSE OF TUDOR

Kings and Queens of England

Owen Tudor *m* Catherine of Valois (widow of Henry V)

Edmund Tudor *m* Margaret Beaufort (great-granddaughter
Earl of Richmond   of John of Gaunt
                                                              and Catherine Swynford)

Henry VII *m* Elizabeth of York (sister of Edward V)
(r. 1485–1509)

Henry VIII *m* 1. Catherine of Aragon 2. Anne Boleyn 3. Jane Seymour
(r. 1509–47)

Mary I   **Elizabeth I**   **Edward VI**
(Mary Tudor)   (r. 1558–1603)   (r. 1547–53)
(r. 1553–8)

Mary Tudor   Margaret Tudor

155

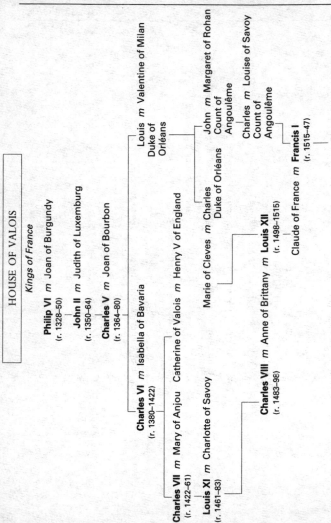

HOUSE OF VALOIS

Kings of France

Philip VI *m* Joan of Burgundy
(r. 1328–50)

John II *m* Judith of Luxemburg
(r. 1350–64)

Charles V *m* Joan of Bourbon
(r. 1364–80)

Charles VI *m* Isabella of Bavaria
(r. 1380–1422)

Charles VII *m* Mary of Anjou   Catherine of Valois *m* Henry V of England
(r. 1422–61)

Louis XI *m* Charlotte of Savoy
(r. 1461–83)

Louis *m* Valentine of Milan
Duke of
Orléans

Marie of Cleves *m* Charles
Duke of Orléans

John *m* Margaret of Rohan
Count of
Angoulême

Charles *m* Louise of Savoy
Count of
Angoulême

Charles VIII *m* Anne of Brittany *m* **Louis XII**
(r. 1483–98)   (r. 1498–1515)

Claude of France *m* **Francis I**
(r. 1515–47)

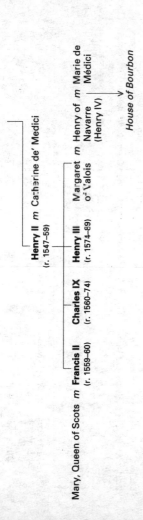

HOUSE OF VASA

Kings and Queens of Sweden

Gustav I Vasa *m* 1. Catherina of Saxony-Luneburg 2. Margareta Leijonhufvud
(r. 1523–60)

Erik XIV
(r. 1560–9)

Johan III *m* Katarina (sister of
(r. 1569–92)   Sigismund Augustus of Poland)

Anne of Austria *m* **Sigismund**
↓   (r. 1592–9)
Kings of Poland

Catherine *m* John Casimir
             Count of Kleeburg

Charles IX *m* 1. Maria of the Palatinate
(r. 1604–11)   2. Christina of
                  Holstein Gottorp

Gustavus II *m* Maria Eleanora
(r. 1611–32)   of Brandenburg

Christina
(r. 1632–54)

Christina *m* Frederick VI
            of Baden Durlach

Frederick VII of Baden Durlach *m* Augusta of Holstein-Gottorp

Albertina *m* Christian Augustus of Holstein-Gottorp

Louisa Ulrika of *m* **Adolf Frederick**
Prussia   (r. 1751–71)

Charles XIII
(r. 1809–18)

Charles X *m* Hedwig Eleanora
(r. 1654–60)

Charles XI *m* Ulrika Eleanor of Denmark
(r. 1660–97)

Charles XII
(r. 1697–1718)

Ulrika Eleonora *m* **Frederick I**
(r. 1719–20)   (r. 1720–51)

Gustavus III *m* Sophia Magdalena of Denmark
(r. 1771–92)

Gustavus IV Adolf
(r. 1792–1809)

HOUSE OF WINDSOR

Kings and Queens of the United Kingdom

George V *m* Mary of Teck
(r. 1910–36)

Edward VIII
(r. 1936)

George VI *m* Elizabeth Bowes-Lyon
(r. 1936–52)

Elizabeth II *m* Philip Mountbatten,
(r. 1952–)   Duke of Edinburgh

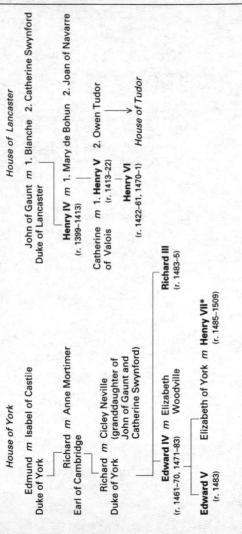

HOUSES OF YORK AND LANCASTER

Kings and Queens of England

House of Lancaster

John of Gaunt *m* 1. Blanche   2. Catherine Swynford
Duke of Lancaster

Henry IV *m* 1. Mary de Bohun   2. Joan of Navarre
(r. 1399–1413)

Catherine *m* 1. **Henry V**   2. Owen Tudor → *House of Tudor*
of Valois   (r. 1413–22)

Henry VI
(r. 1422–61, 1470–1)

House of York

Edmund *m* Isabel of Castile
Duke of York

Richard *m* Anne Mortimer
Earl of Cambridge

Richard *m* Cicely Neville
Duke of York   (granddaughter of
John of Gaunt and
Catherine Swynford)

Richard III
(r. 1483–5)

Edward IV *m* Elizabeth
(r. 1461–70, 1471–83)   Woodville

Elizabeth of York *m* **Henry VII***
(r. 1485–1509)

Edward V
(r. 1483)

*Henry Tudor, grandson of Owen Tudor
and Catherine of Valois

Name	Regnal Dates	Name	Regnal Dates
Charlemagne (Charles I)	800–14	Lothair II	1125–37
Louis I, 'the Pious'	814–40	Conrad III [4]	1138–52
Civil War	840–3	Frederick I, 'Barbarossa'	1152–90
Lothair I	843–55	Henry VI	1191–7
Louis II	855–75	Philip of Swabia [2][4]	1198–1208
Charles II, 'the Bald'	875–7	Otto IV	1198–1214
Interregnum	877–81	Frederick II	1220–50
Charles III, 'the Fat'	881–7	Henry Raspe [2][4]	1246–7
Interregnum	887–91	William, Count of Holland [2][4]	1247–56
Guido of Spoleto	891–4	Conrad IV [4]	1250–4
Lambert of Spoleto [1]	892–8	Great Interregnum	1254–73
Arnulf [2]	896–9	Richard [2][4]	1257–72
Louis III	901–5	Alfonso (Alfonso X of Castile) [2][4]	1257–75
Conrad I [2][4]	911–18	Rudolf I [4]	1273–91
Berengar I	915–24	Adolf [4]	1292–8
Henry I, 'the Fowler' [4]	919–36	Albert I [4]	1298–1308
Otto I, 'the Great'	962–73	Henry VII	1308–13
Otto II	973–83	Frederick (III) [3][4]	1314–26
Otto III	983–1002	Louis IV, 'the Bavarian'	1314–46
Henry II	1002–24	Charles IV	1346–78
Conrad II	1027–39	Wenceslas [4]	1378–1400
Henry III	1039–56	Rupert I [4]	1400–10
Henry IV	1056–1106	Sigismund	1410–37
Rudolf of Rheinfelden [2][4]	1077–80	Albert II [4]	1438–9
Hermann [2][4]	1081–93	Frederick III	1452–93
Conrad [2][4]	1093–1101	Maximilian I [4]	1493–1519
Henry V	1106–25		

Holy Roman Emperors

Name	Regnal Dates	Name	Regnal Dates
Charles V [4]	1519–56	Joseph I [4]	1705–11
Ferdinand I [4]	1558–64	Charles VI [4]	1711–40
Maximilian II [4]	1564–76	Interregnum	1740–2
Rudolf II [4]	1576–1612	Charles VII [4]	1742–5
Matthias [4]	1612–19	Francis I [4]	1745–65
Ferdinand II [4]	1619–37	Joseph II [4]	1765–90
Ferdinand III [4]	1637–57	Leopold II [4]	1790–2
Leopold I [4]	1658–1705	Francis II [4]	1792–1806

[1] Co-Emperor   [2] Rival   [3] Co-Regent
[4] Ruler not crowned at Rome; therefore, strictly speaking, only King of Germany

ROMAN EMPERORS

Dates overlap where there are periods of joint rule (eg Marcus Aurelius and Lucius Verus, 161–9), and where the government of the empire divides between East and West.

Name	Regnal Dates	Name	Regnal Dates
Augustus		Alexander Severus	222–35
(Caesar Augustus)	27BC–AD14	Maximin	235–8
Tiberius	14–37	Gordian I	238
Caligula (Gaius Caesar)	37–41	Gordian II	238
Claudius	41–54	Maximus	238
Nero	54–68	Balbinus	238
Galba	68–9	Gordian III	238–44
Otho	69	Philip	244–9
Vitellius	69	Decius	249–51
Vespasian	69–79	Hostilian	251
Titus	79–81	Gallus	251–3
Domitian	81–96	Aemilian	253
Nerva	96–8	Valerian	253–60
Trajan	98–117	Gallienus	253–68
Hadrian	117–38	Claudius II Gothicus	268–70
Antoninus Pius	138–61	Quintillus	269–70
Marcus Aurelius	161–80	Aurelian	270–5
Lucius Verus	161–9	Tacitus	275–6
Commodus	180–92	Florian	276
Pertinax	193	Probus	276–82
Didius Julianus	193	Carus	282–3
Septimius Severus	193–211	Carinus	283–5
Caracalla	211–17	Numerian	283–4
Geta	211–12	Diocletian – (East)	284–305
Macrinus	217–18	Maximian – (West)	286–305
Elagabalus	218–22	Galerius – (East)	305–11

Roman Emperors

Name	Regnal Dates	Name	Regnal Dates
Constantius I, 'Chlorus' – (West)	305–6	Honorius – (West)	395–423
Severus – (West)	306–7	Theodosius II – (East)	408–50
Maxentius – (West)	306–12	Constantius III – (West)	421–3
Constantine I, 'the Great'	306–37	Valentinian III – (West)	425–55
Licinius – (East)	308–24	Marcian – (East)	450–7
Constantine II	337–40	Petronius Maximus – (West)	455
Constans	337–50	Avitus – (West)	455–6
Constantius II	337–61	Leo I – (East)	457–74
Magnentius	350–3	Majorian – (West)	457–61
Julian	361–3	Libius Severus – (West)	461–7
Jovian	363–4	Anthemius – (West)	467–72
Valentinian I – (West)	364–75	Olybrius – (West)	472–3
Valens – (East)	364–78	Julius Nepos – (West)	474–5
Procopius – (East)	365–6	Leo II – (East)	474
Gratian – (West)	375–83	Zeno – (East)	474–91
Valentinian II – (West)	375–92	Romulus Augustulus – (West)	475–6
Theodosius I, 'the Great'	379–95		
Arcadius – (East)	395–408		

OTTOMAN DYNASTY

Name	Regnal Dates	Name	Regnal Dates
Osman I	1281–1324	Osman II	1618–22
Orhan	1324–60	Mustafa I (2nd reign)	1622–3
Murad I	1360–89	Murad IV	1623–40
Bayezid I	1389–1402	Ibrahim	1640–8
Interregnum	1403–13	Mehmed IV	1648–87
Mehmed I	1413–21	Suleyman II	1687–91
Murad II (1st reign)	1421–44	Ahmed II	1691–5
Mehmed II, 'the Conqueror' (1st reign)	1444–6	Mustafa II	1695–1703
		Ahmed III	1703–30
		Mahmud I	1730–54
Murad II (2nd reign)	1446–51	Osman III	1754–7
Mehmed II, 'the Conqueror' (2nd reign)	1451–81	Mustafa III	1757–74
		Abd ul-Hamid I	1774–89
		Selim III	1789–1807
Bayezid II	1481–1512	Mustafa IV	1807–8
Selim I, 'the Grim'	1512–20	Mahmud II	1808–39
Suleyman I, 'the Magnificent'	1520–66	Abd ul-Majid I	1839–61
		Abd ul-Aziz	1861–76
Selim II	1566–74	Murad V	1876
Murad III	1574–95	Abd ul-Hamid II	1876–1909
Mehmed III	1595–1603	Mehmed V	1909–18
Ahmed I	1603–17	Mehmed VI	1918–22
Mustafa I (1st reign)	1617–18	Abd ul-Majid II (Caliph only)	1922–4